Thoughts of a Sober Heart

By Faith L. Smith

Illustrated by Tamia A. Whiteside & Isaiah A. Whiteside
Edited by Mariah S. Higgins, Khalil S. Porter, Carey Martin, Joseph Saunders, Caleb Ishman, and Faith L. Smith
Writing consultant: Robert L. Watts

Thoughts of a Sober Heart

ISBN: 979-8-218-04082-6
Library of Congress Control Number: 2022913400

Printed in the United States of America
First Edition, 2022
For more information, write to the publisher:
creativelyfaith21@gmail.com

Contents

Acknowledgments

Thank you to my mother for always being there for me and believing in me and my dreams. You were the one who taught me the value of the craft of writing at such a young age, and when I found out that you loved it as much as I did, it touched my heart in more ways than one. We become more alike as the days pass, and I'm forever grateful to God connecting us in the most beautiful way he could think of–a mother and daughter bond. I love you.

Shout out to my stepfather. I never knew what it was like to have a solid male figure in my life. Yeah, I had brothers, but a father figure was something that I lacked for a while until the day you met my mom. Ever since then, you and our family have been through some things, but through it all you still stayed solid with us and you didn't leave. Thank you for believing in me and always seeing our family through.

All the love in the world sent to my siblings. We may fuss and fight from time to time, but each and every one of you knows that when it comes down to it, your sister holds it down for y'all no matter what against whoever and whatever. You never have to question that, and this project right here is for y'all.

This one is dedicated to my nieces Aria and Aryn and my baby sister Tamia. Aria, you're so full of life and so amazing, and I swear when I have my first kid, I want them to be just like you because you're such a beautiful character. Little Aryn, you're not here yet, but I already know you're going to be a little super star. Tamia, us being sisters couldn't make us any closer. We're sisters by chance thanks to God but roll dawgs by choice and it'll always be that way.

Thank you from the bottom of my heart to every person who's ever taken the time out to read my work. Shout out to every person that called dibs on the first copy of my first book. All those firsts better had been the first to get this one (just kidding, but not so much). Thank you for wanting to push me to further my education with my craft and be more hands-on with the creativity part of being a writer.

To every teacher and professor who I've ever had the privilege to learn from and be a part of their class for a semester or year for writing, thank you. From my fifth grade English teacher Mrs. Hawkins to my high school AP Literature teachers Ms. Nicholson and Mr. Carson, and my college professors Mr. Wagenaar and Mr. Byrne, thank you so much. I learned a lot from each and every one of you when it came to writing, and I appreciate you for never letting up on me and always pushing me out of my comfort zone to do my absolute best.

This is for family. This is for love. This is for us. Cheers to that.

Introduction

Love is crazy, man. Love is...absolutely everything any person believes it is and then some. There are so many definitions because the word can be used in so many different ways. Even the dictionary has more than one definition of love. For example, I love writing, but that's not the same as loving my mother. I have a very deep passion for my writing and I do love it, but I love my mother differently. Just like if I loved my partner, that's clearly different than loving your job or a family member. It's a lot of levels to this four letter word, but the level of it that I'm choosing to touch on in this collection is the level of falling so deeply and madly in love with someone you've given absolutely everything to, and then things don't really go as planned like you had hoped. It's also on the level of being on cloud nine and feeling beautifully happy in that person's presence like you won't ever come down from that kind of high but eventually realizing that high doesn't last forever.

Thoughts of a Sober Heart puts emotions and conversations to the rollercoaster of feelings involved with loving somebody and potentially being loved after heartbreak, trauma, and abuse. Usually, there's a specific order in which the pieces are organized in a poetry collection, however, my collection has no order. The pieces picked and written in this collection are as is because when loving and being in love, your emotions are all over the place. Your thoughts and feelings are racing by the second, and sometimes you can't pinpoint what it is that's going on in your heart. The organization, or lack of in this case, speaks to that. Every piece was written in the most emotional states I've ever been in. Some make sense, some don't, but that's also because sometimes love makes sense, and sometimes it doesn't. This is more than just poetry. This is more than me sharing personal experiences of me being in love and in pain. This is me giving a side of myself to the world to relate to and help them work through their own similar experiences.

Now, the title is a different story. The title is actually the title of one of the poems a part of this collection, but I chose to name the entire collection this because I reread these poems several times and I recalled the state I was in while writing them. Everybody, or at least most people, have seen that once alcohol enters a spouse's or a friend's system, true feelings either about you, other people, or situations spill out, and even though these are coming out mostly because of the alcohol, they end up being how these people truly feel. With a sober mindstate, or in this case a sober heart, it's a lot more difficult to be vulnerable and willingly show a side of yourself where you're baring all of your emotions.

I know for me, I'm one of those people who's hard on the outside and not really willing to be open about things I've been through, especially in love. My family knows things, but only to certain extents, so this collection is one that's held very close to my heart. It takes off the mask I choose to wear every day to portray this facade of being okay. This is me realizing that sometimes it's okay not to be okay. I finally release the past to open new doors for the present once and for all.

Thoughts of a Sober Heart will be somewhat therapeutic to a lot of broken hearted women and men, because it takes them to places and spaces they would've never imagined they could go back to healthily to discuss. It reminds people that love isn't perfect. There will always be trials and tribulations, but as long as you make it through to express those feelings in the most beautiful way, you'll end up being okay. You will see another day where you can love in the same magnitude all over again. When that day does come, trust me, loving the right one will come so effortlessly. Think of the bumps in the road as practice for eventually finding the one.

Thoughts of a Sober Heart

Thoughts
Of
A
Sober
Heart

Emotional Rollercoaster

An emotional rollercoaster is probably one of the most insane rides you could ever be on in your life. I feel like it comes right at the start of the heartbreak, and it makes you feel like you're losing your mind. Everything else that comes with it just makes it ten times worse. The revealing of the lies, the hurt and then dealing with all of it after the fact is tough. Heartbreak is blindsiding, because you never see it coming, especially when it comes from the person that you hold so close to your heart. It doesn't feel real, and being hurt with your heart in your hands makes you feel wounded and empty.

I've been on several different emotional rollercoasters. Mine started when I was seventeen. I know because this is around the time I started convincing myself I was capable of being in love. I was a junior in high school, trying to figure out who I wanted to be, and in the same token somehow wanting a relationship. That was probably the biggest mistake I've ever made. At seventeen, I was trying to survive high school, but I was also hit with a lot of outside circumstances that impacted my life mentally and emotionally. This was around the time my family and I had got the news from my aunt that my cousin had just passed away. We went to visit them in Texas for the funeral so they could have support from the family during my spring break that year. I didn't cry when I got the news or at the funeral for two reasons. First, I felt guilty about mourning my cousin's death because I hadn't seen him in so long, so I assumed I didn't have the right to grieve for him. Second, I didn't want to cry in front of my aunt and cousins because they didn't deserve seeing that from me, which was also another way I chose to guilt trip myself.

Anyway, when I was down there, I got introduced to a guy that gave me the much needed distraction from everything that was going on. He was cute and funny, and of course we both made it obvious to everyone else that we liked each other. My mom and aunt even teased us about it. By the time I made it back home, my cousin talked me into giving him my number through her and we started talking from there. Now, I have a great way of disappearing from reality. I'm a storyteller, so my imagination is my escape. I can't escape reality in general, so I try to create my escape. This guy was the escape I created. The only problem was he lived in a completely different state, so at seventeen, I chose to do the whole long distance thing. It didn't work. In fact, it turned out to be a natural disaster.

We argued a lot, mostly because I chose to find a problem with every little thing that he did. If he didn't text me within the time frame I had made for him, it was a problem. If we were on FaceTime and the call got disconnected because of our internet connections, it was a problem. I was finding so many problems because I had so many of my own. A lot that he couldn't fix. Most I didn't even have control over. Technically, I started my own emotional rollercoaster with that one. We ended up being on and off for a while, but just never saw eye to eye. Some days he made me feel like I was on cloud nine. Like the nights where we fell asleep on the phone after having hours of conversation. Or when he used to send me cute little paragraphs throughout the day to let me know he was thinking about me and he would be calling soon. But then there were those days when he made me feel low, *really* low. Like when he didn't answer the phone and texted me the next second to claim he was "busy" but then I found out later on it was because he was with someone else. Or when we argued and he would hit below the belt with certain things he would say about me having daddy issues. That eventually overshadowed the good days. Again, I was seventeen, so looking back, all of this sounds silly, but it started one of the many roller coasters I still haven't gotten the chance to get off of still to this day.

Passionate *(01/09/2021)*

Lay these voices to rest, get them out of my head
They keep telling me I'm not good enough
Would it be better if I could prove it to you?
I'm always moving for you

Make me forget
Forget that I'm not perfect
Forget that I don't deserve this, or you
Convince me that I'm more than something to be used

Give me a rush
I don't care if that means you're my drug
I'll throw back a few shots for you
Pop a pill, watch me as I swallow you

Once all of me stops breathing
I start losing purpose with the seasons
When the seasons change, my feelings change
When feelings ain't the same, I turn back to the pain

Like the feeling of loneliness in a room full of people
It's the ones you love most that hurt you the deepest
Nothing can take the pain away,
so why not just bathe in it?

I'm passionate, about the love I give
I can't handle it, if it's given back to me
That's why this is endless
I don't know where my head's at

I had to lose myself, in order to prove myself
I guess I'm just passionate
Why does it have to hurt so bad?
I know it's just who I am
I'm passionate

Conversations *(01/09/2021)*

Set me free, from broken promises
Like, "I'll never leave you alone.
I'll stay faithful and I'll always come
back home."

Don't you sit there and tell me
things I've heard before.
Like when you say, "You're beautiful,"
but you used that one before.

Spare me the long winded explanations,
on how I'll always be your baby.
Mariah did it best, don't you ever
disrespect a legend.

Forget an understanding.
I'm so damn misunderstood, that I lost everything
I could, now I wish somebody would,
ever try me like I'm not the best they ever had.

Forget your feelings.
Sometimes I wish you never did this
to me because I pity your other bitches.
They're gonna end up just like me.

You know you had the realest.
Now you're subjected to invest in females
that ain't even invested in who you are
and what you believe.

Instead I have to watch and let them take credit,
for the man that I created, because you set me free.
You thought your other options would give you something
that you felt was better than having me.

Weren't you the one that said,
"This time I'm really in this. I won't
ever leave again and I'm here whenever
you need me."

Funny how that changed so quickly.
It's funny how you treated me that way,
and now you're wondering what happened to me
Like, "What the hell has gotten into me?"

I'm the one that's been paying for your indiscretions.
I'm the one that's up late nights with tears in my eyes,
the stains laying on my pillow case.
You were never there to wipe them away.

Forgive me for making you the blame.
I guess it's my fault for trusting somebody
that ain't never gon' change.
No matter how much I feel for you,
I know for a fact shit between us will never be the same,
and you're the blame for every time you played with my name.

Perfectly Imperfect *(01/11/2021)*

I'm taking my time, this time I'm doing it right
Enough with the lies, I refuse to deal with it this time
You told me I wasn't good enough, so I wanted to prove myself
To you, when you looked me in the eyes while I laid with you

You said I wasn't beautiful, so I kept wishing to be someone else
I would dream of what I would be like with long hair flowing down my back
Ass wider than a field of jasmine and clovers
Maybe then you would want me to be your lady, over and over

I wish I could take it back
The times I dimmed my light just to distract you from my flaws
But then I would have to face the fact
That it wasn't meant to be with you

If I didn't go through what I went through with you
I wouldn't have moved on in hopes of bettering myself
While preparing myself for the beautiful love I deserve
The love I know deep down inside I will always be worth

If I didn't have that piece of me
That still sometimes plays make believe
Or that piece of me that overcame everything
I wouldn't be me

**Shout out to Savanna Cristina's Self Love joint. I listened to this song a lot when I was going through my healing process and it's helped me so much.*

Final Destination *(01/24/2021)*

This wasn't part of the plan, but yet, here I am
I wasn't supposed to stand for anything less than my demands
Yet somehow I fell for the master plan of this sick ass game of love

Silly of me, to think I learned from the last time
After countless times of sleepless nights and teary eyes
You'd think I'd stop giving you and love a try

For some reason I still believe it's out there for me
I won't stop until it's proven to me
That it's just not meant to be for you and me

Welcome, to Heartbreak Station
Your ticket should tell you this is your final destination
The death of your heart happened as soon as you entered the station
Long live the brokenhearted assassinations

All aboard, the Bitterness Train
Because after all of the pain, the anger will take you some places
Sometimes it's hard to tell if you're gonna make it

How much of a fool can I be?
To actually think, you would be different
Your generosity took me by surprise

At first I didn't know if it was a disguise
But all of a sudden in a blink of an eye
You started telling me lies and staying out all night

I'd call you, you wouldn't pick up the phone
Then we'd get together and the energy's all wrong
Like this was your only way out and I was your pawn

When we go out, your eyes shamelessly wander from woman to woman
When I ask you what the deal is, you claim that it's nothing
But then I catch you exchanging numbers–I knew it was something

You said you were cut different, not like the rest
Somehow you were just the same, just not at its best
A little more hurtful, but a lot less of the man I thought you would be

Lie To Me *(01/29/2021)*

If you can't love me, say it anyway
I find that it's easier to be with you even if you can't stay
So say the things I want to hear
I may not need it, but I want you to be here with me
Stay with me, through the hard times
There might be too many to count, but sometimes
I try to see if you're strong enough
For me, be only for me
Especially if I'm giving my all, baby, I need you to see me
Just lie to me, tell me everything, even if it isn't true
I know fairytales don't really exist, but I'm a believer in the myth of me and you
Lie to me, it helps me sleep at night
It almost feels as good as your hands caressing my thighs
Despite the demise that lies between our eyes
You're mine and I am yours, but you're mine rightfully so
Nobody knows, but that doesn't mean I'm not gonna let them know
Promise me you won't go, even when you don't love me anymore
Because I don't want to be alone

**Queen Naija was like the national anthem to my broken heart. I could never not play a song by her during the times of me going through breakups, and when she came out with Lie To Me, that chorus was on repeat in my head and it was a wrap from there.*

Separate Spaces *(01/29/2021)*

So it seems, love doesn't live here anymore
All we have are memories, the rest is at the door
If only I could remember, around the time in September
Where we started to believe that commitment we could not achieve
And whatever remained between us became history

I used to think we were inseparable
Wherever I go, you would too
Now we spend our time in separate spaces
You choose your side, I stay on mine
I can no longer look into your eyes when you look into mine

Is it still only me or is your mind starting to wonder more?
Like, "What can I get into outside of me and you?
If I choose her, would she ever have a clue?
Is this better for me, or should I stick with you?
Why is it so hard for me to choose only you?"

You used to be there for me
I'd never have to call too many times
Because before I could even think about picking up the phone
You would answer, no questions asked
I was at some point becoming your priority

What's on your mind?
Would you mind sharing it with me?
Sometimes I don't know if you're in the mood for me
Your colors change like the sunsets we once shared
That's the reason why we live in separate spaces
You're moving in your direction and I'm following mine

One too many times I tried to coincide with your life's schedule
But actions proved I was the one more invested in you
I thought caring for you like I never did before would make things different
But once again I was proven ain't nobody really cut different

It's the same story, just new characters
Sometimes I wish we never crossed paths because everything after us would be no more
I'm done bending over backwards for little boys that ain't true to form
They just become a waste of time, and I'm no longer made for that life
I've already let my love for love die

Until I find somebody that can actually get it right

I'll move with myself and hopefully one day
Somebody will show me it's worth it to keep hope alive

Conversations with the Poet: Story Behind "Lie To Me"

Lie To Me of course was inspired concept wise and title wise by Queen Naija. You know how people remake their favorite songs? That's kind of what I did but in poetry form. Her song with Lil Durk has a very catchy chorus, and it's something that not only stood out to me but it stuck with me. The first couple of lines are what actually went on repeat in my head. It goes, "Love me good and lie to me. Don't want broken promises, don't want apologies." Shout out to Queen, because I played that song over and over again when it first came out. Hell, every now and then I still bump it just because. This poem took me back to that song and specifically those lines of the chorus.

These poems are not written too far apart, and they all have their own little emotional backstory to them. However, *Lie To Me* specifically is when I just was at a point where I just wanted to give up on love. I was desperate in the situation I was in at the time. I wanted what I wanted. It didn't matter if he was ready for what I was ready for or not. That was selfish on my part. I didn't want to know the truth. If you can't do right by me, cool, just don't admit it. If you don't love me, I don't want to hear it. Back then, I just wanted somebody, and it's crazy how the mindset of a person can change in the span of ten months because now I see that as settling in the lowest form. I was over it then, and I just wanted to be loved my way.

Before this new situation, it was like I was in back to back moments of disappointments. From getting my heart broken from somebody who was in a completely different state to getting betrayed by somebody who ended up being my first to dealing with the after effects of somebody putting their hands on me. It seemed endless, and I thought it had finally come to an end the day I started being with this new situation. Don't get me wrong, the situation had a lot of beautiful moments, but that was my thing. It was just a situation. It was nothing more than that, and I knew I deserved a lot better than that. I just settled for what it was because I chose to convince myself it wouldn't get any better than that. In reality, I deserved to have a partner. I deserved to be the girlfriend, the priority, the potential wife. You know? He just didn't see it that way.

Lie To Me is like the cry for help addressed to that new situation. While writing this poem, I was writing it as if he was sitting in front of me and I was saying these words directly to him. It's sad to say now, but then I was really that desperate. In my mind, I had found the end all be all for me, and still to this day I see something in him that he doesn't see in himself. He didn't feel as though he was meant to be loved. Unfortunately, you can't force people to look at themselves the way that you do.

In a nutshell, I just wanted that connection, but where I went wrong was I wanted to be loved in a way that I wasn't loving myself. If I'm not loving myself as hard and as much as I invest in trying to get someone else to love me, how can I expect the person that I want to be completely in love with to love me just the same? Therefore, although this poem was very emotional, it was a wakeup call to myself to get my shit together and spend more time with myself instead of chasing after someone else.

Nevermind *(02/06/2021)*

It's been a long time coming, but we need to stop frontin'
We started out lovin', all the kissin' and touchin'
Then you switched up, I guess it ain't that easy does it
Even though you're fine and you're mine, I know we're running out of time
We can't catch up to the outside, because people think we're together
When really this is hard to define
Nevermind, about all the things that I said when you were locked out of my heart
I know I said it wouldn't be easy on me if we ever grew apart
But it wasn't hard to convince myself you weren't shit from the start

Actions speak louder than words
Don't tell me you love me and end up showing me the worst
The deeper we go, the more that it hurts
This back and forth gets on my nerves
I would rather be alone than empty with you

So nevermind about them messages about how I miss you
I was ready for you, but that was the issue
So much for us being a team
How could you do this to me?
How could you let me believe that I was your everything?
Nevermind about the love that I gave you with my trust
You abandoned every part of my existence
It's hard for me to get out of my feelings about you
Every time I get to contemplating us, I get confused

Still to this day, I can't see myself with anybody else but you
I don't want anybody else to see me through
I gotta let you go, but in the meantime I'm gonna let you know
That these feelings I have for you, at the moment I just can't show

So nevermind about that anniversary that we never got to see
That was a sign it wasn't time for us to do our thing
I would've given anything to be by your side
Despite the demise, I would've been down for the ride
Through the pain of it all, I wouldn't let me fall
What you did, I know I said I could forgive
I could never forget, how you put me through some shit

So nevermind about the time that I gave you
I tried to save you
Turns out, I'm the one that needed saving
Somewhere down the line, you ain't hesitate to press decline
So nevermind

Trust Issues *(02/16/2021)*

When you tell me that you're coming home late
My mind wanders to different places
When you can't give me any explanation
It's clear you're with her with no hesitation
In my mind, I know I'm the only one
Love dealt me a bad hand, so I'm fucked up
I don't trust, and I can't have us

Somewhere down the line
I'm gonna accuse you of being with somebody else
Even if she doesn't exist, in my mind she does
In my mind, I'm not good enough for you
In my mind, I'm this close to losing you
I'm too far gone, but I'm still choosing you

Tell me the truth, do you have secrets?
If something ever happened, would you keep it from me?
I'm drowning in love with you
Even if this could be beautiful, I can't give it a chance
I can't feel *it* again

If I was meant to be loved, it wouldn't be this way
Are you hearing me?
Don't plead to hear from me, please be here for me
I'm crying out for your help, don't leave me by myself
This is getting too hot, so I might as well save myself

Where *(03/01/2021)*

Pieces of me, lay by the ocean
Why don't you dive in deep, in slow motion?
Give your all in just one night, no pressure, baby
I'll take it all and I won't fight
I'll be your canvas in the sand
Take you swimming in the deep end
You don't need your life jacket, ain't no saving you
When the sun goes down, I'm in the mood
Whenever I want it, I get it from you

Tell me where you want it, I'll jump on it
Anything I do, don't try to control it
Let me catch the vibe while I ride you into the sunset
Don't try to hide, you know you want it
So stop playing games and push up on it

Visions of you, come inside my head
This is more than just sex, it's a movie at best
It's hard for me to forget
With my legs high, ass right, these back shots are more than a ten
Late nights after date nights we do it again
I'm coming on slow, where you like it the most
Got me so focused, you split me wide open
I'll throw it back by the ocean
Tell me where you want it

**This piece is the only one of the poems in this collection where I play on the the sexual side of love. It's sexy but it's innocent, and I love the fact that I'm more comfortable with freely expressing that side of myself.*

Want U 2 Fly *(03/06/2021)*

Patience, you've been patient with me lately
Frustrations, we face them on a daily
I know it's hard to deal with me on your own
I never said it would be easy, just believe me
When I tell you that I'm wrong, forever leaving me, baby
My colors change faster than the seasons
It ain't that simple, but all I ask is that you work with me

I've been messed up, from the past
All the shit he did fucked me up bad
I want this to last, don't go too far out of grasp
Between you and me, let's be free outside of my head
I know it adds stress, but if you bare with my mess
You won't regret taking a chance on me

I understand that this could be for the moment
My heart can't take it, but I'm willing to be open
Although you got me right where you want me
I gotta put into focus that things could come to an end
Even though I want them to begin, over and over again

If there was ever a time you regret the day we met
I want you to fly higher than you ever did
Touch the sky, don't you ever hold back
Don't just chase your dreams
Make them become your reality
Try not to do it because you think you owe me
Do it because you know it's always been your destiny

Reminisce *(03/06/2021)*

Hooked to your bullshit
Why'd you have to do this?
Why did I have to be so foolish?
To believe that you could never do this, to me
I thought love was supposed to be patient and kind
I thought love didn't boast because it wasn't allowed to do the most
I guess that just goes to show you
That they could even put it in the bible
Yet you still wouldn't know how it goes
Even though I've had my time, somehow the lies still get to me
See, you don't know what love is
Since you didn't put up a fight
You'll never know what love is
You let me walk out of your life
Time can only tell where we really stand
Even though that only gives me more time to hate you
On the ground where you stand
Common sense makes it easy
To see that you were playing me
All the times you let me sit alone at night
You had me wondering why I let myself get to you
Answering questions I should've been hooked to
Standing on your broken promises
That you made me fall through
Who am I kidding when I say that you tried to love me?
I loved you, when I didn't love myself
I could never hurt you, because I'd rather love you for my health
It hurts to stay, but I can't let you go
I would rather be with you and miserable
Than by myself and all alone

**Summer Walker's Session 32 inspired parts of this poem. When she says, "You don't know what love is, if you don't put up a fight," that's where I go back and forth with the concept of loving someone just enough to get by but not enough to fight to keep them in your life.*

Dream Girl *(03/17/2021)*

One in a million, I'm one in a few
You said before me it was hard to get through to you
You said you're used to having girls for free
At the drop of a dime, you could call them fine
Then what came after that was easy
Never had you experienced a woman like me
That's what you said to me
"How is she better than anything I've had before?"
"Why is she everything I've been praying for?"
Those were the questions that you had about me
"Damn, that girl's my dream, now I have to see
what this will mean for me."

Maybe it was the thrill of the chase
In the beginning you were grateful
To be blessed to be standing in my presence
You said whenever we were together, it felt like heaven
Getting me was hard, but you made it clear you were playing for keeps
I went in circles with my heart about you and what we could be
I knew I was your dream girl, and you convinced me
That you would do everything in your power to keep me
That's what you said to me
You told me, I was your dream

The second I chose to choose you
The switch up in your attitude just wouldn't do
I put it all on the line for you
Then your dream turned into something that couldn't come true
I was right there in front of you
All of a sudden this became something you couldn't do

Maybe it was hard for you to believe
That everything you dreamed of, you found it in me
Or maybe you weren't ready to be with someone
Who was ready for something more than you could actually give
Either way it goes, you still tried to play pretend
Now my heart is left shattered and the pieces are blowing in the wind
It was easy to forgive, but what's hard is that I have to forget
Somehow the pain is still as fresh as it could get

I shed my tears over you
I went into a dark space, I was so confused
You dreamed of me, but I was a believer in you
Then you just had to be a disappointment too

You know it's bad when you're crying after the well goes dry
You harbor so much pain, you can no longer feel it
Instead, you use it as your defense
Then you hurt the ones that wanted to see you happy and content

I even had my mama tell me you were my biggest setback
To this day, I can't get that out of my head
That day, I was brought back to my senses
God came down and talked me off of my cliff
He said, "Daughter, let me straighten your crown.
You're unique, special, and strong enough to hold it down.
You're my chosen one, and you're forgiven.
If you have listened to the words I have spoken,
your days moving forward will remain beautifully opened."

I did my reading, that turned into my healing
Once I started at the beginning, I realized there was no ending
I let go of my past, and stopped saying I wish I never had
made the decisions that led me down certain paths
Without them, I wouldn't be able to grow
I detoxed from the fuck boys, and now I have a healthy glow
I might've not stayed your dream girl, but there's something you should know
I came across a real man and he's showing me how this is supposed to go
I'm not your dream girl anymore

Conversations with the Poet: Story Behind "Nevermind"

I get pissed off a lot with the person I'm involved with, but this particular poem was post the end of the situation I was in a year prior with my first. It took me a very long time to let that anger go, and for me, writing has always been therapeutic. This poem was written in March of 2021, and this is November of 2021, which means eight months ago I was a little bitter. Actually, a lot bitter. I can't lie, I thought I was the shit when I wrote this poem because I feel like out of all the poems that I've written, this piece is like some type of ultimate diss track or something. Mind you, I'm in a completely different mindset and emotional state than I was eight months ago. But since we're talking about this poem, I was still going through it.

The situation with my first ended on the worst note ever. It turned into a block party, meaning I completely blocked him from every part of my life. That was the closure. There attempted to be a conversation, but it went completely left, and when it went left, at the time I had no problem blocking this person on every form of social media that I shared with him as well as his phone number. Because of how it ended, I had a lot of animosity towards the situation. I had a lot to say to him that I wanted to say in person, but I couldn't because I purposefully blocked him and there was no way in hell I was allowing myself to go backwards.

That's when I turned to writing about it. I had a very unhealthy way of dealing with my emotions. The way I dealt with everything was simple. I just didn't. It's been that way my whole life. Somebody dies, you move on. Somebody hurts you, you stay strong. Don't speak about it. Don't take time to heal. Just pick up where you left off and move on. I'm getting much better with expressing myself as an adult and a woman, but back then I held everything in. If I felt some type of way about something, whether it was big or small, I held on to it for the longest. The problem with that was I would hold on to it for so long that I would let everything pile up. Then out of nowhere I would just explode. The actual problem at hand would eventually turn into the fifty million other problems I refused to address and openly express myself about in those moments.

This piece got real personal for me, and what I was thinking about while writing this poem was what my mother said to me when I came to her for advice about the dude. I remember being over my mother's house one day and I came to her crying about the guy that I tried to one up my first with in the poem after completely ending our situation. My mom was basically telling me that I'm better than what was going on. Men are men, but there are lines that shouldn't be crossed. She said that every man has problems with their emotions, but that's no excuse to be nonchalant, and at the time he cared about our situation as much as I did. He was just having trouble showing it.

The conversation transitioned into my mom bringing up what I went through with my first, and she was brutally honest, which was something I needed to hear. She told me that this new situation is nothing like the old one, and that the old one was one of my biggest setbacks I've ever had thus far not only because of what I went through, but also how I dealt with it after it was all said and done. My mother does her best to keep her say out of me and my siblings' personal relationships because she doesn't want us to feel some type of way, but hearing that from her, the only thing I could do was agree because she was absolutely right.

I didn't handle my first well at all. He was my first everything, so I was all broken up. Him choosing to be with other girls and then having the audacity to look me in my face and lie about it every time while manipulating me into thinking I was the one tripping fucked me up. Especially since I chose to make our situation my first serious encounter at that time. I remember I cried like the biggest baby for days the first time we actually called it quits, and I was still living with my mom when this happened. One day she got tired of seeing me on that same spot on our couch in the living room crying my eyes out, so she decided to make me get up and go with her to run errands. That was one of the first of many times she dusted me off and straightened my crown when it came to me and the boys that I dealt with. She taught me to know my worth at a very young age, but I lost sight of that as I grew up, but she brought me back to the light every time. However, this last time was different because once I shut out my first, I forced myself to act like nothing happened.

There's no love loss at all with this person. It took me an entire year to get to a place after everything was all said and done to be okay not only to write about it but also to talk about it without getting pissed off or sad. Actually, we're on a somewhat cordial level. I've been wishing him nothing but the best since day one. Just because some things happened, doesn't mean I have to switch up. It just means I know there better not be a next time. Maybe one day we could genuinely be friends without having feelings for each other, but for right now, I'm just going to keep it pushing and doing me.

Come Closer *(03/18/2021)*

From a distance, I may look like your fantasy
Gracing across the field of life
You may think, “She doesn’t show emotion, she doesn’t leave herself wide open.
Why does she want a better half?”
From around the way, I may look like a star
That you could wish upon a star, and never wonder who you are
You’d be amazed that I could go that far

If you come closer to me
You’d be surprised to see me wearing my heart on my sleeve
It’s made of glass, for the world to see straight through
I wear emotion like a style that’s never out of season
If you come closer to me, you’d see the twinkle in my eyes and realize
I’m not a dream, but rather the reality–that’s me
The dream actually lies behind what could be the possibility of me
Come closer to me, there’s a lot beneath what you actually see

From across the ocean, I’m a fairytale
I’m Cinderella through whatever, you don’t have to worry about the details
Before the clock strikes midnight, I’ll be your best yet
The colors are changing the sky, but the bond is never changing between you and I
Under the moonlight, I’m everything for you, and to you
You’re my Prince Charming, and here you’re seeing me through

If you come closer to me
You’ll find I’m not perfect
I got bad days, mostly sad days
I hold it down, all around
I’ll be your biggest fan while giving you all that I can
Sometimes I can’t stand, on my own, but I’ll always stand, for you
If you choose to come closer to me
You’d see I yearn for the impossible
I find myself wanting what I’ve never had before
Don’t come any closer to me if you’re not ready to set me free

Lola *(04/16/2021)*

She dances in the city, a lover at night
The pole is her master and she is your dancer
But only for one night
Here, she feels alive–the only time she feels all right
When the morning comes, she prepares to put up a fight
In the club she writes a different song
There she uses her assets to get what she wants
She gives out a couple dances
Sometimes she convinces the men that she's ready for romance
She knows she hates the club
She only goes because she knows her emotions won't show
This is her home, where her heart is locked away
Tears stain her pillowcase but on the pole they're kept at bay
When the lights go down, how does she make everything okay?
You might be a big tipper for her but where are you
when she needs someone to come to her rescue?
In the club, she's your star
At home, she lives too far
Away from her vice, the only thing she can suffice
Black and blue, the colors he decorates her with
How could you notice a survivor with hands all over it?

Stuck on You *(04/18/2021)*

It feels like yesterday, when I gave you your walking papers
I still can feel the pain, of seeing you walk away
It's funny how all the important dates, my mind can't erase
Like the first time we got acquainted
You saw me and couldn't look away
I wanted to know your name
Then I hooked you on to my game
From there I was making the biggest mistake
You showed your love in the beginning
Made me feel like I was always winning with you
It turns out I was never really *with* you
I thought there was something about you
That made me want to call you my forever with no ending
An always repeating beginning
Then somehow things had to change
That's when you started with your games
I'm the one that was getting played
Your love was just a phase
That's why I can't seem to understand
How I wanted you to be my man
You let me down to the very end
Even thinking back to all you did
I'm stuck on you, that's why I can't forgive

**Shout out to Giveon. Stuck On You is my favorite song by him. I love this song so much that I had to pay homage to it with one of my pieces.*

So Over It *(04/19/2021)*

What I give must be irrelevant
It seems if you give just a little bit, you become too much to deal with
If you put your heart out on the line, you become too much of a bitch
Apparently somebody is out here telling people not to catch feelings
Like that's something too hard to deal with
God forbid it, if you end up being a good woman
If you hold somebody down, they'll still swear that you're frontin'
Don't show them something they've never seen before because they'll go runnin'
Don't be the best they ever head because it'll still mean nothing

I'm so over it
I don't know why I go for it
They get me every time when they show just a little bit of interest
I think they're just a little bit different and then they decide to switch it
Like, "Bitch, you really thought I was the realest? You thought you had me
for the long run and this was gonna lead to marriage and children?
You thought what we shared was special and endless. It's too bad
but you gotta know you're the one that did this."

It's sad but I've been through enough
Although it hurts, what's coming your way is worse
When you get fed up just a little bit
You start giving them a taste of their own medicine
That's when they really start to feel it
Like, "Why are you out here trippin'? Why are you so distant?"
It's when they really lose you that they get in their feelings
All of a sudden they start to act right and claim now they're really in this
It's a shame you gotta be put through hell to get to forever
I can no longer stand in this type of weather
Before now, it seemed you would never let up
I'm so over it, but I gotta keep my head up

Tables Turn *(04/19/2021)*

I'm putting on my makeup, and slippin on that little black dress
I know it's your favorite, and I know you're under stress
This time, I'm not wearing it for you
Instead, I'm going out with the girls, and maybe I'll catch a rendezvous
I'm wearing those heels, that you said gave me a little extra sex appeal
Maybe I'll show someone exactly what they made you feel
You're out here forgetting anniversaries
Then you had the nerve to come for me about not answering your phone calls
Come to find out, when you don't answer mine
You're making somebody else's bed your home
The games people play get them left all alone
Luckily, I'm staying right here, just for you
If you think I'm not gonna have my turn, know that I'm coming for you
How would you like it if I shared a night with someone else?
What if I gave myself to someone without your consent?
When the tables turn, there's nothing that can be said
When I have it my way, there's nothing left to pretend
Your actions will eventually come to an end
When I do what you do, that's when you know you lost a real friend

**One day, I was listening to Tank's Maybe I Deserve and this is kinda like the response to what he was talking about in the song. I would never step out on my spouse, but when they do it to me, in the back of my mind there becomes that question of, "What if I do you how you did me? How would you feel and what would you do?" So this is me touching on that "what if" and letting the guy know I'm doing him a favor. I could do it back to you, but I won't because I know how I move. Just know in the back of your mind that if I did, only one of us will get hurt and I promise it'll never be me.*

Time Changes *(04/21/2021)*

I’ve been staying focused
I’ve been on my grind, it’s my time to shine and I know it
I used to stay down for too long, but now I’m over it
I’ve found my crown, not looking down
Took a seat at my throne, I’m no longer leaving myself wide open
I don’t have time for you to double back again
You see I’m going out more just for the hell of it
I’m posting pictures just to show myself I’m the shit
It was never to spite you because no thoughts of you ever crossed my mind
If I’m being honest I never think about that phase of my life
I’m moving on so I can’t meet with you tonight
Unless you plan on making reservations for four tonight
Then again, you could never have enough room for me, myself and I

Time changes circumstances
For you, I was a sexual gain, your healing advance
You abused the privilege of me revealing my sacred temple
You treated it as just something to revisit for fun
If it didn’t work out with the other one, you were calling asking if I was still yours
We had arrangements but you still tried to make it seem like I could be played with
Now you were the one to catch feelings and I’m letting you know
That time changes those who evolve, and I’m not the same
You should probably keep your distance because nothing else between us remains

Conversations with the Poet: Story Behind "Come Closer"

This is probably the most important poem I've ever written that I've included in this collection. It's important because it's not only very vulnerable, but it's probably the realest I've ever been with myself and the person I was writing it to. The state of mind I was in at this time–mind you it was a month after the first set of poems was written–I was just trying to figure everything out for myself and my personal life. Mentally, I just wanted to regroup and get to the first step of moving on in some kind of way. I feel like the pain of heartbreak in any form will always be there somehow, but to me it's all about what you do with it. I chose to put it in my writing, which was the therapy and wake up call I needed for myself.

Come Closer is me reflecting on who I am as a woman and as a person. It's a warning in a way to the men out there who are trying to pursue me post heartbreak. I'm basically saying that from a distance, being involved with me on the surface is everything and more, but once you come closer, you see there's a lot beneath the surface that you may not have bargained for. This is no way at all telling men to stay away from me, it's just letting them know that if you do decide to approach me, this is what you should be ready for and this is what you need to know. If you can handle that, great, but if not, you need to not even think about looking my way.

I remember sitting down and writing this one. I was listening to an instrumental. This is when instrumentals started to heavily influence my writing. I couldn't write without one, so I found this instrumental to this particular poem, and in my journal it's written in a completely different way. However, for the sake of this collection, I decided to edit it and expand on it a little more. When I wrote this one, I had my candles lit. Everyone knows my writing atmosphere has to have a good smelling candle involved. I was sitting in the middle of my living room floor of my studio apartment, and I was just going in, and I didn't stop. I was locked in from start to finish. I wrote it in one sitting and it evolved into what you just read today.

Of course now I feel completely different. I'm much more comfortable and open to revealing what's beneath the surface of Faith. I know I'm not perfect, and in this poem I acknowledge that very wholeheartedly. I have absolutely no problem admitting my flaws, my faults, or what I've done wrong. Best believe I wasn't always like this. I'll argue you down about me being right even if I know everything that came out of my mouth was wrong, but I've grown from that. With this poem I was just trying to reveal myself a little more and add a softer side to who I really am. I do come off hard as well as intimidating. I've even been told to my face that I'm emotionally distant and closed off, so this allowed me to put those assumptions I give out to people to protect myself to rest.

Thoughts
Of
A
Sober
Heart

Honest Conversations

The first eighteen poems are a little out there emotionally to say the least. There's a lot of anger, a lot of sadness, and honestly, a lot of bitterness embedded in each poem. Of course you can see that I was angry. I was mad as hell that I went through the stuff that I went through not only with my first love in college but also with every situation after that. I had gotten to a point where I actually had hate in my heart for my first, and anybody who knows me knows I wasn't built to hate anybody in any way. I was taught not to hold grudges, but during that time, it was hard for me not to hold anything against my first. Writing was a way for me to release that grudge towards him. Therefore, a lot of the poems within these first eighteen and even some of the ones you'll read after you get through this section have a lot of aggression, pain, and burden carried within them.

I just turned twenty-one back in April, and as you can see the poems were written at the top of this year. Eight months ago, these were my feelings towards these people. Not just toward these situations, but also towards love and towards myself. I felt like I was chasing after something that was never meant to chase me back. I ended up being that cliche. I was looking for love in all the wrong places, as H.E.R would so flawlessly put it. I wanted attention. I wanted affection. I wanted to be loved, and I settled the score with whoever I thought was giving it to me even if it was the bare minimum.

What I completely didn't understand at the time was why I had to play games with the one I was involved with for him to take me seriously or even for me to express myself to him without him shutting down on me. Why did a man have to damn near lose me to see how much I actually mean to them? Of course I understand now that a real man–that's down for you and that's gonna ride with you past the wheels falling off–would never put you through the obstacle course of loyalty and love to be with them.

So during these times of me going through these roller coasters of emotions, I was going crazy. I was nowhere near myself and I started acting out of my character and doing certain things that I would never do if I was in my right mind. It started when I got into my very first almost serious relationship when I was nineteen with my first. The guy I was involved with in college. I will never forget this night because I knew he was playing with me the moment he came to my event. For my final project in my creative writing class, my professor wanted us to do a reading of one of our poems that we included in our final profolio to the class. We could invite friends if we wanted to just to widen the audience and have a fresh perspective to introduce to our work. I invited the guy.

He showed up, but the whole time, his phone was blowing up. It was an unsaved number and the number was sending him paragraphs at a time, which of course meant when it came to him that somebody was going off on him for not answering the phone. It was my turn to go up and I said my little poem and he's in the back recording me. When I step away from the little podium setup, I go back to my seat thinking this man is about to sit through the whole event and we're gonna kick it afterwards. This number keeps blowing him up and he's trying to do everything in his power for me not to see these messages. He's tilting his phone every time I look his way, turning his brightness down. Everything. Clearly making it obvious that he had something to hide in that moment. He wasn't that good since I caught a glimpse of the messages, so he did all that for nothing, and I was pissed. Why would you come to my event with that bullshit?

Long story short, he ended up leaving. He decided to leave my event that I invited him to. My whole attitude changed after that for the absolute worst. I had the biggest feeling that it was another female that was blowing him up. Way later down the line I ended up finding out my gut feeling was true, but in that moment a different energy took over me. We had the option to stay after we read our poems to the class to mingle and do extra stuff to get to know everybody, but I was ready to go. The whole time I was sitting with one of my homies in the class. I'll never forget her because in this particular situation, she was the realest homegirl that I've ever had at that school.

Just a little side bar–at the time I was going to Valparaiso University. It wasn't a predominantly black school, so it was very much a culture shock for me since I was coming out of being a part of a predominantly black high school. I was really standoffish. I didn't talk too much unless I had to. I always kept to myself. Basically, I was a completely different person personality-wise than I am now. There was a lot about that school and the people in it that didn't sit right with me, but Lera was one of the few people that I met and thought was cool at that place. Other than that, I really didn't associate myself with anybody.

Anyway, this girl in my creative writing class had my back. We'll call her Lera. If you ever read this, I wanna thank you for holding it down this day because we ended up meeting to go to the event for our final together. Since we came together, I explained to her what had just happened with the dude, and she was the one that was like, 'We can go over there if you want to. If you go, I have no problem going with you.' I was pulling up regardless, and I didn't really think she was going to do it, but when I said I'm going to pop up, she went with me. In the meantime, I'm texting this man and he's not responding, he's not answering my phone calls. Nothing.

Luckily, Lera ended up talking me into going back with her to her dorm. Her roommate was gone so for a little while it was just us. She let me cry to her, she let me vent, and she was a really good friend that night. Neither one of them probably remembers this story. I know for a fact the guy doesn't remember certain parts because he had no idea all of this was happening outside his room, but it was about to go down. I'm not even built like that but I was about to be about that life for that night only.

I say all that to say that it's moments like this that I was thinking about and reminiscing about that I held on to for so long that spilled into these poems. I have no problem talking about this stuff now because it doesn't make me angry anymore. I can laugh about it. I was foolish to say the least, but I found humor in the fact that I was something else when it came to how I handled certain situations. With anything that requires me to dig that deep, especially with this kind of project, I have to tap into those moments and revisit how I felt to make these emotions come off as raw and fresh as possible.

Thoughts
Of
A
Sober
Heart

Old Wounds

Old wounds take time to heal, and in order to heal, you have to recognize those wounds first. As you can see, a few months ago I had a lot of wounds I wasn't ready to face yet. However, in order to understand my emotional state fully, you have to know how I got there. I've dealt with a lot of things in my life at such a young age. I've dealt with some serious self-esteem and self-love issues. My self-love was zero at one point for a long period of time. I had no idea what it meant to love myself, and I also had no idea what that looked like. I had my mother telling me and showing me, but I didn't know what any of that meant to me at such a young age. I struggled with accepting who I was flaws and all because of how I saw myself, which was less than. My mother taught me how to walk in my power with my head held high. She reminded my sister and I every day how beautiful and strong we were. It's just that when I got older and started venturing out into the world on my own, I lost sight of that. I let a lot of people's opinions be the reflection I chose to see when I looked in the mirror.

I also had very little self-confidence. I wasn't comfortable in the skin I was born in, and some days I'm still not. I was self-conscious about every little thing about myself, especially how I looked. Caring so much about how I looked really impacted who I was as a person and how I was shaping myself as a woman. I remember some days having mental breakdowns if my hair didn't look the right way. My hair was known for being bone straight and silky. However, my natural hair is really thick and kinky. If I didn't achieve that silky straight look every day, I felt like I wasn't pretty anymore. I knew kids would make fun of me if I didn't look how they expected me to. I got to a point where I wanted every detail about myself to be so perfect that I started cutting out all the hairs on my head that were out of place and not laid down like they were supposed to. I won't lie to you, I hated my hair. I just started going natural almost a year ago. Before that, being natural scared me. I was used to the perms to get my hair straight and using a flat iron or a hot comb in case I needed a touch up. Then when it started breaking off from the perms and me not properly taking care of it, that made me even more insecure because I had started to get less and less flexibility with different styles when it came to how I chose to wear it. I felt like part of my beauty was in my hair.

It was an unhealthy obsession to be everything to everybody look wise and even life wise. In school I was a straight A student, and after a little while it had gotten to a point where if I made anything less than that, I was a disappointment in certain people's eyes that I wanted to make proud. Like my teachers, mentors, and friends. I was relying on approval from the wrong people without even realizing it starts with myself. I made a lot of mistakes trying to impress outside people. Everybody makes mistakes, but if Faith makes one, it's one of the biggest mistakes ever made because she's not supposed to make mistakes. If Faith has a bad day, she's looked at a certain way because there's no reason Faith should be having a bad day because she's not supposed to have bad days. It was a lot to keep up with, especially as a child. The outside world expected a lot out of me that I felt like sometimes I was being pushed way too hard on. I understand people expect great things out of everybody, but the level of vigorous tactics in place to push me towards that greatness was not helpful to me mentally at all.

I was also bullied in school, *hard*. The kids at school growing up would come at me crazy. This is a materialistic world, and for whatever very wrong reason, you're exposed to name brand meaning everything at such a young age. If it wasn't what I was wearing, it was my hair. Like I said, I hated my hair growing up, and I only hated it because the other kids teased me about it. I had really long hair as a child until I got to kindergarten. One of the girls at school was jealous of how long and thick my hair was and one day in class, they put some sticky stuff in my hair that wouldn't come out. My mother had to cut it out. When she cut it out, she had to cut out most of my hair. The cut made my hair uneven and later down the line it started being even more damaged from the heat and everything. It hasn't been able to grow back right since. Sometimes the bullying was physical. This one boy used to really beat up on me. I remember one time we were on the bus and he tripped me on the bus floor in my new off-white pants. I was excited about these pants because I looked so cute and my mom had did my hair real pretty and I felt like I looked good. When he tripped me, I busted both of my knees. The blood from my knees and the dirt on the bus floor combined got my new off-white pants dirty.

My family is also a little left field. They betrayed so many trust factors it's a shame, which is why the family circle I do associate myself with is so small. My outside family has abandoned my immediate family in moments where family should've never been divided in the first place. They've taken advantage of my mother on multiple occasions, and then they have the nerve to come around like nothing ever happened and we should be willing to help them out when they need it. Aside from that, there are a lot of deaths that I've experienced that happened back to back. As a child, I stayed in a church dressed in all black because there were so many people that died. My immediate family was always the rock to the rest of the family in these times. After a little while grieving wasn't an option, you just had to be there for the rest of the family and be the shoulder everyone could lean on. Being strong for everybody else was our job, even when I was barely standing on my own. Even when I didn't understand why it had to be me. I think the icing on the cake will always be my father.

My father decided he didn't want to be a father when I was eight years old. After giving my mother three kids–me being the oldest of those three–he decided it was finally time to go back to his wife and other grown children. He was building a home with my mother for eight years, and then just snatched it away. My mother will always be the greatest superhero that ever lived in my eyes because she raised five kids all by herself with no financial or emotional support from not one person, including the fathers, and she did amazing. She put all five of us through high school, and we all to date graduated with honors. Most of us went off to college, and those who didn't found a secondary trade in what they loved to do. My father lived up the street from us all four years I was in high school and never even picked up the phone to say hello. My mother never blocked him from being in our lives. She never took him to court for child support, because she saw there was no point in forcing him to be a part of our lives because his actions were showing he just wasn't interested.

I think the moment that really sealed the deal and made me move on from ever having a relationship with my father is when he inserted himself back into my life right before my grandmother on his side passed away. He called me and I didn't answer because I believe I was at work when he did. He ended up leaving a voicemail that basically was telling me how sorry he was about not being a vital part of my life. He was hoping we could spend more time together and get to know each other, and at first I was hesitant because I had been down this path with him before. After phone conversations and him checking in on me from time to time, I decided to give him a chance. I felt like he was proving he wanted a real opportunity to try and be my father. One day I finally got the courage to ask him to meet up with me so we could have a face to face conversation to air everything out and try to move forward with each other. He ended up turning me down and then the next time I tried to reach out to him, I started getting no answers which led to him blocking me from his social media pages and my phone number.

Adding all that on top of my personal love life, all of it kinda shaped how I viewed love and how I went about getting that. I was lost, bruised, and confused. There were no positives for me to look up to at that time, so I forced myself to create my own. I think that's why I love movies so much, especially romance movies. The dynamic and happy ending really touches my heart, and ever since I was a kid I've been trying to mimic that perfect fantasy to my reality. I realize now that's impossible, but I tried my best to convince myself that it was possible.

Love's Heartbeat *(N.D)*

I wish I could write a letter to the hands of time,
Maybe then it could stand still.
The longer I look into your eyes, the more I can see,
That it's you that makes love feel so real.

If love had a heartbeat, it would skip every second.
You are the center of what makes everything I feel just like heaven.
If it had words to speak, it would be speechless.
All the things that you do would make love feel fearless.

I could write this forever, and make it into a song.
It's you who makes the melody that I sing to all night long.
Please don't be afraid of the love I have to give.
It's the only thing I want to give to you.

Keep Me In Mind (N.D)

Inspired by Cardi B's "Be Careful"

I'm giving you all I got, and I promise you I'll never stop.
You can walk out that door tomorrow, but I'm still giving you all the love I have inside.
Treat me real special because you ain't about to find anyone else,
That could love you without judgment,
Or care for you without complaints.

Just keep me in mind, when you stay out all night,
And a pretty little woman tests you with all her might.
She'll bat her eyelashes and twirl the ends of her hair,
And she may even ask if you have someone out there,
Especially when she doesn't really care.

Just keep me in mind when you share that first kiss.
Does she hold a smile in her eyes, or is it just on the lips?
Is her touch as soft as mine, or is it just bliss?
Does she love you like I do,
Or is she just a quick fix?

Just keep me in mind, because I'll always be the best you ever had.
Who else would be that foolish to stay with a man that bad?
You ain't make me feel like I was your one and only,
And no matter how hard I tried, I was always competing with someone.
Too bad you weren't the one, but I found another man, and he knows that I'm just enough.

**When I heard Cardi B's Be Careful, that put me in such a mood of being ready to light my first's ass up. Before him, Long Distance did have somebody else on the side, but dealing with my first was the first time I had a situation where there was more than one girl involved. Cardi ignited the anger I was already starting to feel towards College Dude, and that gave me the courage to put a voice to it.*

My Diary *(N.D)*

Also included in Valparaiso University's Fall 2018 edition of "The Lighter"

Try to keep my secrets,
And I'll keep yours.
We could even trade thoughts,
And offer ourselves just that much more.

Normally I wouldn't suggest this, but I've been cut wide open.
My soul has been exposed, my clothes have been torn,
My mind has been picked apart,
And this has become another form of art.

I try to keep my promises,
Now you should keep yours.
Share this with no one,
Not one soul.

Because you are my diary.
You created the lines to the pages
My pen sweeps over ever so gently.
You're the lock to the key I always carry with me.

Don't tell anyone,
Not even my soul.
Keep all of my secrets,
Even the ones I haven't told.

**Alicia Keys is a musical genius. The piano in certain songs she has always sticks out to me, but My Diary is one of those hits where I felt like it was speaking to the lover and writer in me.*

Someday I'll Love Faith Smith (N.D)

Winner of the 2018 Academy of American Poets Award

Faith, close your eyes. Envision
the shadows of your mother's love.
Taste the bittersweet tears you left
in the river banks along the Mississippi
ruins. Leave it all behind. Put your
hand in mine, and let's walk along the
shore and leave our footprints buried
beneath the sand.

Faith. Faith, I hope you're listening. Take
the auburn leaves we collected at the
Boston Harbor, and allow them to whistle
into the wind like a spirit descending
beyond the heavens. Let them be no
more. Your mother will always be
your mother. Like cupid resting on the
crescent of a full moon, there will never
be another.

Take the emerald stone you left
in your father's pool, and let it drown
in the blood of the dead. Your father is
your father when you're not there. He
might've forgotten, but your mind is like
an empty field filled with dandelions
blowing in the wind. Memories float in
the air, and your father was never there.

Faith, open your eyes. Let them follow the
dusty trail that leads to a mirror holding
your reflection. Smile. Your heart is an empty
bird's nest yearning to find her young. Let
this pass and you'll learn that everything
lost is left in the sunset.

Matters Of My Heart *(N.D)*

Is it wrong to yearn for love?
I've created a pledge for relationships.
For every tear, I want passion.
For every crack in my heart,
I want a kiss,
But not just any kiss.

I want a kiss so soft,
It washes away the hardness of life.
I want a kiss so gentle,
It reminds me that men aren't supposed to be so rough.
I want a kiss so deep,
It caresses my soul in a way that makes me forget the pain.

When I say pain,
I mean the pain of an eight-year-old girl wondering if
her father loves her back.
When I say pain,
I mean the pain of watching your mother wonder if life
loves her back.
When I say pain,
I mean the pain in your chest when you have to watch the
one you love walk away without reason.
When I say pain,
I mean those tear stains on your pillow case that come alive at night
because that's the only way you can put yourself to sleep.

These are the matters of my heart,
I crave to be cradled past the grave.
I need an escape,
I'm sophisticating in the middle of the street where no one
can see me.
Soon, my heart will be displaced.

Maybe *(N.D)*

Also featured on the Wattpad app

Lately I've been thinking, been hoping and wishing,
That maybe one day we could be something different.
It could be something to begin with, so tell me are you with it?
Because baby I've been thinking, baby are you listening?
I got this feeling that maybe I've become addicted,
To love, love, love, lovin' you now, but only for right now.
I don't know what to do, I'm confused and I can't choose.
Tell me if you had a choice, who would you choose between me and you?

A lot of maybes in my ear, like maybe we should be here.
Maybe you deserve and I deserve the chance that we have near.
I know it's such a long shot,
I know this ain't all you got.
I know that maybe I'm too far out, but I've put myself out there,
So baby this is all I got.
Just be patient with me.

Look into my eyes, make me feel alright.
Maybe I shouldn't be here, maybe this isn't as real as it feels.
Maybe I should've stayed in the back where you couldn't react to me.
Maybe I'm not really all that, just something to distract you from reality.
Something is telling me that it's fine,
But the look on your face tells me I'm out of line.
Maybe I love the feeling of your arms around me.
Maybe I'm just busy living in this moment with you, baby.

To Me, From You (N.D)

Hey, it's me again.
I'm writing this from
the corner of my heart
where you reside.

Your room now has a bed
that's not meant for sleeping,
but it reminds me that
you're still here with me.

There are pictures on
the wall that capture
every moment of the love
we once shared.

Although it might not
had been love to you,
to me it was the closest
thing to my truth.

My truth is that I'm
in love with you,
and I don't want
to lose you.

I can't love what
doesn't want to be kept,
and I can't wait for
what's already left.

So the door to your room is
closed, sealed by a lock
with no key to reopen
Pandora's box.

I send this with
the love I once had
for you, and no remorse
for the guilt you feel.

Conversations with the Poet: Story Behind "Someday I'll Love Faith Smith"

This is probably the most personal poem that hits the closest to the core of my heart that I've ever written to date. It's crazy because this won an award when I was in college in fall of 2018. This was literally my pain on a page that I tried to express in the most complex way possible three years ago. It's one of the few pieces that I have that addresses my father. Anybody who knows me knows that my father was one person you would rarely ever hear me talk about. I'll tell you all the beautiful stories in the world about my mother all day long, but my father was forbidden territory. Only a select few people that have crossed my path over these twenty-one years of me living know the story of my father, and back then I did it that way for a reason. I didn't like talking about what happened, and this particular poem forced me ten years later to open that box with the emotional burden I was carrying after everything was all said and done.

This poem is addressing myself, as if I'm staring in a mirror commanding myself to do these things I'm saying, and it's absolutely the complete essence of a self-love poem. When I was eighteen, as I already mentioned, I had the worst self-esteem issues ever. I had little to no self-confidence, and I was just a mess as far as seeing myself as worthy and beautiful. My professor in my creative writing class gave me the concept for this poem. He showed me different examples of poems that had been written following the same format and he said I should write one and submit it to the Wordfest competition at my school.

I love writing about anything. All I need is a concept and it's go-time from there, so when I read the different examples, I went back to my room on campus that I paid to stay in a couple nights out the week since I was a commuter, and I just locked in. I knew I would have to dig into a place I had never been before, and that place was the forbidden territory of the subject of my father.

In the poem, I don't address just him, I address what he did. I basically say he forgot that he was supposed to be my father, and I kinda scrape the service when I say, "Your father will always be your father, but only when you're not there." In a way it was a dig. Although my father did what he did, I would never disrespect him on a level of me not acknowledging him as my father. However, I will address how I feel in a way that I feel respectfully conveys that.

This poem is rooted in the pain that I felt when he left. I can only speak on what I know of. I know he was there for the first eight years of my life, and I know he left. The details in between are kinda all over the place because there are mixed stories, but certain things I know for sure that I remember because I was there was the day he left. I actually wrote a short story about this that mirrored the reality of what actually ended up happening. When my father was in my life, nobody could tell me anything. I don't think I was ever truly a daddy's girl to begin with. I'm definitely my mama's baby, but I loved my daddy almost just the same. He saved me from most of the few whoopings I did get when I was a kid. I was the first girl that he had with my mom, and I think that father-daughter connection alone is what bonded us from my birth up until the time he left. I remember the days when we used to do stuff together as a family. Back then, our household was big on wrestling. We used to put the mattress from either my brothers' or my mama's bed in the middle of the living room floor and the whole house would just wrestle together on the mattress. My brothers would be jumping off the couches like they saw some of the wrestlers do on TV. We used to get my daddy real good.

I remember this one time we tried taking a road trip as a family to Milwaulkee and that ended up going all wrong. My siblings and I were little kids, so we got on my mom and dad's last nerves. We had to go to the bathroom every five minutes, we were complaining about getting car sick, we always wanted something to eat. We had a lot going on, and Milwaulkee isn't even that far of a drive but with five kids in the backseat, it was pretty far for my parents. If I remember correctly, I think one of my parents ended up getting mad that we were doing the most, and we ended up turning back around and not going to see my aunt and cousins who had lived out there at the time. Those are the things I remember about my dad actually being around, but the one memory of him I'll always remember clearly is the day he chose to pack up and leave us.

I was eight years old, and at this time it was my parents, me, and my other four siblings. I had three brothers and a baby sister. We stayed in this two bedroom apartment. The boys had their room and the girls stayed close to my mom in the other room. My dad worked a lot at the steel mill, so the memories I do have are from the rare times he was actually home. If he wasn't at work, he was most likely asleep. When he wasn't at home with us, he didn't allow my mother to take my siblings and I outside. We later found out that was because he didn't want anybody associated with his wife and other children to see us walking around. It was a controlling situation at times, so I barely got to go places when I was growing up. I couldn't see too much of the outside because my dad never let me. He wanted to keep his secret family tucked away as long as he could.

The day he left, I was sitting on the edge of my mother's bed, and I was watching an episode of *Spongebob*. I don't know what was happening that day, but I don't remember any of my siblings being in the apartment. I do remember my mother yelling at my father at the top of her lungs. She was so upset with him and I knew that he knew he had messed up pretty badly because he was quiet. Then after that all I remember is his shadow appearing in the doorway of my room. When I was a kid, I thought my father was a giant, so I always had to literally break my neck to look at him.

I didn't look at him, but I could feel the tears running down my cheek. In the corner of my eye I saw him with a suitcase in one hand and he was trying to say bye to me and hug me with the other. I didn't say not one word to him, and he just left. Once it came to light that my dad was living this double life, that's when his wife got involved. She found a way to get in contact with my mama and told her if she ever saw me or any of the rest of the kids he had with my mom in the car with him, she was gonna ram the car with us in it. She went as far as making the daughters that she had by him, which are my older sisters, pretend like they wanted to create a bond with us so they could basically spy on us for the wife to ensure my dad wasn't keeping in contact with us. She doesn't want my dad reaching out to any of us, and he actually listens to this woman. Later down the line, he ended up remarrying somebody who purposefully destroyed three innocent children's lives.

I felt like absolutely nothing to him after that. I felt like he didn't fight for me. I felt like he didn't want me to be a part of his life. I felt like he didn't want me to be his daughter. For a while, I was lost because of that. I battled those feelings and emotions and that whole situation by not facing it at all. I harbored everything, and ten years later they just came spilling out. That's when I realize how much it actually hurts. This poem made me realize how much my father hurt me. That started the next thirteen years of the never ending cycles of similar pain. A lot of people see a father leaving as the normal when it comes to the Black community, but it leaves very deep wounds that no one chooses to discuss. He chose to leave me, my mother and my siblings for a woman who wanted to risk the safety of his own children because of him. I wasn't enough for him at the time, and that started the first of many traumatic heartbreaks and betrayal I've ever had in my life.

If You Can Hear Me (06/26/2019)

If you can hear me, I hope your heart still skips beats
to the sound of my voice.
I hope when you listen, your body feels like the brink
of summer's eve at sunset.
I hope my words create shivers down your spine and dance
across your soul like a rebirth to the world.

If you can hear me, tell me I'm wrong.
Tell me the pain is only temporary and my love was never lost.
Tell me I'm right, for opening my heart to your unconditional conditions.
Tell me that as long as you can still hear me, we'll be holding each other
in the sand by the fountain of youth.

If you can hear me, I hope this is enough.
I know I hold a heavy burden and life doesn't really give me much luck.
I know I swore off giving, because I never received, but from you
I've gotten more than I'll ever need.
If you can hear me, I love you.
My heart beats to the rhythm of your drum, and until you stop playing,
your drum will be the only one I hear, but only if you can hear me.

Goodbyes at Sunset *(06/26/2021)*

You caressed my face with the warmth of your touch,
and captivate my love with your adoring heart.
Never in a million lifetimes would I have thought to say goodbye,
because the care you gave made me think this would last all my life.
God called you home, just before sunset,
so you hold me until he finally takes your hand.
You grace the water, look over your shoulder,
and with your eyes you tell me I'm everything you ever wanted.
I hold my tears as I watch you disappear at the horizon,
and your face glosses over the sky with a smile.
You tell me it's not goodbye, because you'll see me tonight in my dreams,
and there you will kiss me like smoke rising through steam.
Now I watch the sunset faithfully.
I wait at the beach for you to appear right next to me.
I know you made me promise not to cry for you,
but that doesn't mean I don't long to be given a chance to start all over with you.
So until we meet again, I'll always meet you at sunset.

**Grief is never easy. I've lost way too many good ones in my life. It's a process that seems to never end. Prayers up to anyone that's ever lost someone. You're not alone and my heart is with you.*

Emotions *(06/30/2019)*

If I told you I was afraid to love, would you believe me?
I know I give you the runaround whenever we talk about our feelings
Yeah, it's true, this shit ain't easy for me
I've been brokenhearted too many times to count
I shouldn't put it all on you
I got trust issues, so when you say you got me, I don't know what to believe
I get a little hesitant but I still don't want you to leave
I can't have it both ways
I'm pushing you to the edge but at the same time I'm begging you to stay
When it comes to emotions, I can't express them
Ain't nobody ever taught me how to handle them
For so long I've been wishing for love, but when it's right in front of my face
I do my best to fuck it up
Something tells me this love shit will be hard to grasp
I'm a handful by myself, but I'll make it last
It's easy for me to write this on paper or in a text message
When it comes to phone conversations
I'm always stressing about what to say
I can't do face-to-face
'Cause I'm scared that you might actually wanna be my bae
I thought I was ready to give my heart to you
With all I'm holding on to, I'm barely here
So when I try to argue with you, it's intentional
I feel like when drama gets in the mix, it's easier to walk away
I'm too good at goodbyes because after that there's nothing left to say
I've watched too many walk out that door
So before you leave me, I'll beat you to it
It might be good for awhile, but just know there's nothing more to it
I dream about being the relationship type
I bet it'll feel good to be in someone else's arms for a night
Maybe you're right, I need to deal with my past
I walk around with a load, so how the hell we gon' last?
Is it bad that I never made love before?
That I never committed?
I've done a lot of things, and now I'm looking back like I wish I never did it
I don't know too much about anything pertaining to me and you
What I do know is that I'm shooting for the stars and there ain't no holding back
I might've missed out on some opportunities to love
This next one's gonna last
I'm gonna put in the effort and seek out to get what I never had

You Got Me *(06/30/2021)*

If we get to live to see the day that the world is over
If we get to live to see the days when we get older
I hope to be standing, right here, in front of you

If we get to live, to see forever
If we can stand together through any weather
I hope that I'm right here, holding you

'Cause it's only you, for me
You got me, and I got you
I said it's only you, for me
Baby, you got me, and I just wanna be close to you

Runaway *(08/24/2019)*

I'm a caged bird that can't sing,
a figure of speech that has no meaning,
a forbidden dream with no ending,
and a happily ever after that's nonexistent.

I've earned my freedom,
but it's under restrictions.
I'm a young woman that seems to never reach her peak.
Climax without sex, I'll have to finish myself.

I can't find my song.
I lost it as a young girl.
Actually, it was stolen from me,
so I can't dance to the rhythm of just anybody's beat.

Overrated *(11/27/2020)*

When it comes to love, I'm a little jaded
I confuse lust with genuine connections that's outdated
I'm afraid, because the deeper you look into my eyes
The faster you'll take my heart away
Am I to blame?
I wear my emotions on my sleeves
It's hard to explain
I fall fast, but I'll love you harder
I won't let you in but I want you to pull me closer
My mind will never be with you but I want you all in
That's why relationships are overrated
I'd rather suffer in heartbreak than push aside my fears and be patient
These men all have the same intention
Once they get my body, that's it for them
When it comes to love, it never loves me back
That's why this that shit's overrated

**Shout out to Blxst for his song Overrated. This is kinda a response to what he was saying in his song with a twist.*

Perspective *(11/29/2020)*

I wish I could see me, the way that you do
From right where you're standing, you have such a clear view
I know you've been patient and I see you, I promise I do
Sometimes you forget, baby, I've got issues
I'd be a fool, not to bare them to you
Even with everything that's happened, you still see me through

Why can't I love me, the way that you do?
There's something that you see, from your point of view
That I find hard to believe, I promise it's true
If only I could love me, the way that you do

Sometimes, I get a little insecure
Sometimes I wonder, if my heart is truly yours
I have those days, when I'm not too sure
Then I'd have something to say, that'll cause you to walk out that door
Baby, I swear I'm not to blame, but when it happens
You show that you care for me, no matter what happens

Why can't I love me, the way that you do?
There's something that you see, from your point of view
That I find hard to believe, I promise it's true
If only I could love me, the way that you do

Conversations with the Poet: Story Behind "If You Can Hear Me"

All right, so, I didn't meet my first, College Dude, until the fall of 2019. We didn't get involved with each other until later in that season. However, a couple months before this during the summer, I had this little summer fling. I had a year of college under my belt. I was a fresh nineteen, and I'm not gonna lie, I was feeling myself. Around this time, I had reconnected with one of my childhood best friends for the first time in years. We had the biggest falling out ever. It got really deep for petty reasons. We got over it, but at the time we were on two different pages. She was attending and working at Purdue Northwest over the summer and I was just trying to enjoy my last few days of freedom before going back to school to start my sophomore year at Valpo.

My best friend is more of the party type. She likes to turn up, she likes to let loose, and at the time, I was literally clean-cut, super fearful of the party life. Whenever I was around her, she somehow always found a way to get me out of my shell. One weekend over the summer, she invited me to come out to kick it and party and just have a good time. I went, and she introduced me to one of her friends. He flirted with me the entire time. My best friend had a boyfriend, so they were doing their own thing. I don't remember ever meeting him over that particular weekend, but I know after she introduced me and her friend, we hit it off instantly. Me and her actually ended up getting into it again because I ended up spending the whole weekend technically with the guy instead of her.

In the end he ended up playing me, so that was kind of an I told you so moment for her that I deserved, but around the time that I wrote the poem, there were conversations we were having about moving things forward. He was trying to figure out what he was gonna do as far as where he was gonna work after everything that went down with this girl that was hating on him and my best friend the whole time I was there. She was actually their roommate and she stayed going out of her way to get them in trouble in some kinda way. Long story short, I was trying to help him while also trying to figure out if we were gonna continue to see each other, and he was on board. Then out of nowhere, he just went ghost. No contact. No warning. Nothing. That hurt me only because I was dumb enough to catch feelings when it was just supposed to be something fun.

So, *If You Can Hear Me*, is basically almost like writing a letter to Summer Fling with no address to send it to, and me just hoping he remembers how I made him feel. It was crazy to say the least, and now looking back on it I laugh because I really put stock in a temporary situation. I was nineteen, I thought I knew what I was doing, and I felt like I was ready to experience what I thought could be something special. It turned out to be the complete opposite, and I jumped into something that wasn't supposed to have my emotions involved. I didn't know how to detach my feelings from something that was meant to be casual because I'm a lover at heart, and I'm always chasing after a relationship. I fall extremely fast, which is one of the biggest issues I have when it comes to love. It's not a joke when I tell you I wear my heart on my sleeve. It's the truth.

Thoughts

Of

A

Sober

Heart

Old Wounds: The Breakdown

These 14 poems for this section are giving you a glimpse into how I got to where I'm at now emotionally with love and relationships. The first half I dug up seven poems from the archives, which is why they have no date. I'm not too sure when exactly they were written. I know the year was possibly around 2018 or before because I found a few of them from past submissions I did my freshman year of college for different scholastic magazines and newspapers. I'm just not entirely sure the date it was written. I gave you a taste of my thought process and emotions from a more recent perspective of where I'm at with the hurt and everything towards the first half of this year in the previous section. Now I'm giving you where it somewhat started.

I chose to format it this way because I feel like when you meet a person, you get the version of them that they are right there in front of you. You have no idea what they've actually been through to be like they are now, whether they're the sweetest person in the world or the coldest person you've ever met. You don't know the backstory until you turn the page and continue to turn those pages. From there, that's when you start to dig up the backstory of that person. That's when you start to see exactly what shaped that person and what molded their current thought process.

Before the first time I ever had sex, before I started seeking something serious with a guy, I was already in shambles. I had the burden of my father weighing heavily on my heart. I had trust issues from friends that I would have never thought would betray me in the ways that they ended up doing me. I was breaking a few hearts of my own because I didn't have an understanding of what it meant to be loved properly by a good guy. I can admit that I let a lot of good ones go because I was afraid of what was right since I was so used to everything about a connection being wrong. I was fresh off of graduating high school when I first really got into writing poetry because I started realizing that was one of the few outlets I gave myself to let out all of my emotions at once. However, one time, it came to a point where writing wasn't enough and I started having these mental breakdowns every other day in private. At one point I started relying on alcohol and pills to just relieve the stress and take me away from the pain that came with everything that I was going through. Then when it came to being around people, I would act like everything was perfectly fine.

Harboring ten years of bullshit, and then finally letting it out at eighteen to now, I started feeling like I was mentally insane. When I used to stay in the dorms when I was in school, I used to have panic attacks in my dorm room when I was by myself. Those were the times my emotions really got the best of me. This ended up happening all the time out of nowhere. I didn't give myself a chance to deal with anything until I got older. I will give credit to one of my old friends Tara because one time I had a panic attack so bad, I thought I was going to end up in the hospital. Luckily, I had enough strength to call somebody, and the first person I called was Tara because I know that's something she used to suffer with. She ended up calming me down just in time for me to be okay enough in that moment, and I'll never forget her for that.

At one point in my life I was suicidal. There was this one time where I tried to overdose on pills. I suffer from migraines, and I had gone to the doctor to explain what was going on. The doctor prescribed me some medication for it. I was only supposed to take them when the migraines felt like they were starting to hit me, but it transitioned into me taking them every single day. It had gotten to the point where I couldn't sleep or couldn't function without taking those pills. At that particular time I felt like I was crying out for help with every outlet possible to get that help but cripled myself from receiving it properly. People would see the sadness in my eyes. People would see how tired I was. People would acknowledge that I wasn't the same anymore, but I never let anybody know what was truly wrong with me. I tell my mother everything, but I never let her in on that part of me because one thing about me, I never want to put something else on my mother when she's already been through enough. I want to lighten her load, not add to it. I want to now take care of her since I'm able to, so my mother barely knew about any of this. I tried to get myself through this because I felt like other people had problems way deeper and bigger than mine, but at the same time now that I have a better understanding of the importance of mental health, I see that's something that should be held at a high value. That's why I just wish in those times I would've spoken up and gave myself the help I knew I needed.

When I started relying on those pills, what saved me was actually College Dude. Although our situation didn't work out, we'll always be homies. I feel like if we only developed a friendship before the feelings and sex came into play, we would have never lost contact for such a long period of time. One thing he always held me down with that I do commend him for is always making sure my mind was straight. He always wanted me to be okay. I don't remember this day, so I'm going off of the story he told me. He said I called him in the middle of me taking the pills. He said I was going on about not being happy. I was crying and carrying on. However, he ended up talking me off my ledge. He said he got pulled over by the police on the way to me because he was speeding to get to me. When he got there, he said I was high off the pills and ended up having the biggest breakdown ever in the passenger's seat of his car. I never ask people to hold me down because I feel like expecting them to always be there for me is selfish of me, but sometimes you have to have those people to hold you down. Sometimes holding it down for yourself is too much, and if you're the only person holding it down for everybody else, who's holding it down for you? That's why I go so hard for my mom because she's one of those people who always holds it down for everybody else. I thought I could do the same.

I say all that to say, I needed way more time to myself before I even thought about doing anything with anybody. I felt like if I put all my energy into a relationship and all the focus on the dude that I was involved with, I didn't have to think about anything else. However, that only magnified my issues in the end. Don't get me wrong. I'm not saying what has happened between me and the situations I've been in weren't fucked up. However, I am saying and taking full responsibility for the fact that I had my faults within these connections as well. It takes two to tango.

Thoughts
Of
A
Sober
Heart

Honest Conversations Pt. 2

Love isn't as complicated as it seems, because it all depends on who you're dealing with. For me, I've only ever been in two situations that I took seriously. I've only been in love once out of those two situations, and that was with College Dude. He was the first and the only person who completely had me all in, and I feel like we just have something between us that just will never die out. Whatever that flame is. I don't date to waste my time. I want marriage, kids, and a solid foundation at the finish line. I want us to grow together. I don't want all these things instantly, but if I don't see myself building with you toward these things, I don't want to be with you. That's why it disappointed me when everything was all said and done with all of these situations that I settled for a lot of bullshit because I wanted to be loved so badly. Chasing after something that I needed to find within myself first took more out of me than it should have.

I didn't know what it meant to have shared values when it came to my partner and I. My foundation is God and my family. God was only in the core of one of my relationships. We prayed together before every meal we shared together. We prayed together through hard times. We gave thanks with each other in the midst of the beautiful blessings we both individually and collectively received. Unfortunately, down the line we ended up straying away from that because I was too invested in forcing the situation to be what I wanted it to be while he was invested in solely looking out for himself. I wanted the picture-perfect relationship I saw on social media or TV and he was focused on his career and his music, rightfully so. My priorities were absolutely in the wrong places at the time. I made him my number one and I'm not sure if I ever held a spot on his list.

I don't address this a lot, but at one point in my life, I was with someone who had chosen to put their hands on me constantly. I wasn't raised to ever see that. I never witnessed anybody putting their hands on my mother because they knew better. My mama didn't play that. My mother raised my sister and I to be strong and to never let a man walk over us and treat us less than. She also raised us to never let a man put their hands on us.Therefore, when this happened to me, I was stuck. I didn't know what to do, because the question of what if something like that happened to me never really crossed my mind. I was ashamed that I was going through something like that, only because I felt like I knew better, and this was one of those things where since I cared so much about how people thought about me back then, I knew if people had found out, they would have looked down on me in the worst way possible. I knew I had let myself down in a way I felt like at the time I couldn't come back from. I never went to my mother because I felt like I had to figure it out on my own. I put myself in the situation, and I didn't want anyone else involved just to get hurt as well.That made me convince myself that I deserved what was happening to me. After a little while, I knew I had to get out of that situation before it turned into me not being able to make it out okay. That wasn't love in any form, but I accepted it because that's what I felt like I had to at that time.

Thoughts
Of
A
Sober
Heart

The Current State

The current state of my heart? That's tricky. I feel like it changes every day. I go back and forth between wanting a relationship and wanting to just be alone because I feel it's safer that way. I'm definitely a romantic at heart. I want my happy ending in the most beautiful way possible. I want that for myself and I see myself getting that, but at the same time, I'm so tired of getting hurt that I'm not really even trying to be bothered. I'm single at the moment, and honestly, I'm just doing me. I'm not involved in anything serious to where I consider myself dating to see what's out there. I'm just chilling. What comes my way, comes, and if it ends up going away, oh well. I'm literally by myself, and for right now I like it that way since I have so many other things I'm putting my focus into. What I didn't know how to do back then that I kinda gained knowledge along this healing journey now is how to put myself as the number one priority. I'm investing in myself and rediscovering who I am, what I like, and just enjoying every single part of myself that makes me who I am as a person and as a woman.

Lately I've been keeping things straightforward. No strings attached. I haven't met anybody yet that's caught my attention to the point where I'm willing to even think about getting attached again. I'm not saying I'm on some type of strike from love and relationships, but I am saying this time around I'm not chasing anything. I'm just letting whatever God has meant for me come to me and let it be from there. Of course you have to date or at least meet new people to see what's going on in order to allow something to come to you, but right now I'm okay. You never know, someone could change my mind sooner than later, but until that day comes, I'm chilling.

I've learned what to look for in a man as well as what to seek out from a man. What I used to look for in someone wasn't what I needed them to be. Therefore, I started coinciding what I needed from a man with what I wanted to have everything come together. So today, what I need from a man is patience. I am in the process of healing, but even outside of that, I know I'm not the easiest person in the world to deal with. A man can definitely handle me because I keep the peace and I bring the peace, but every now and then I do have those off-the-wall moments where for no reason I catch an attitude or I get sad or I'm just not myself. A man with patience would know to just take his time with me. I thank God I'm developing patience within myself because Lord knows I was the most impatient person ever created.

I also need someone who's kind hearted. I like to see how a man treats people outside of myself, because you can be the perfect gentleman in my presence, but when we go out to a place like a restaurant, you could possibly treat the waiters and the hostess like shit. That doesn't go together and that's definitely a big turn off for me. When I go out in public with somebody, I'm paying attention to how they treat strangers on the street. How they treat the janitor. How they treat and react to children. How they treat and talk to women, especially the ones in their family. If he's talking to his mama crazy, there's very little chance he's coming at me correctly. All of these little things reveal who this guy is as a person and as a man.

I want somebody who's spiritual or at least open to understanding my spirituality. God is the head of my life. I practice prayer and the Word daily. He's in everything I do, and if He's not accepted or a part of the life of my partner, he's not meant for me. I would never force God on anybody I'm involved with, and I don't judge people who have opposing views to Him. However, for me, that's where my roots are. That's who I was raised to put my faith in thanks to my mother. It definitely would be a deal breaker for me if God wasn't the center and the foundation of the relationship, or at least accepted to be a part of it. You can have opposing religious views, but if you can't accept and respect the fact that I follow the Word of God and I'm a believer in everything that He is, it's just not for me.

I love a man that's spontaneous. I get excited when I'm being exposed to things I've never seen before. I'm currently exposing myself to first-time experiences, so the spontaneity of my partner would just add to it. Let's travel to places unheard of. Let's create moments at the drop of a hat whenever we choose to go out. Let's just have fun together. We only get one life and only God knows how long it is, so let's make every second of our days together count.

Finally, I need understanding from a man. I've been very misunderstood my whole life, and I believe the only people that are a part of my life that do understand me fully are my mother, my sister, and College Dude. Sometimes parts of my family don't understand me. My former friends didn't understand me. That's why understanding in a union is important to me. It's a gateway to clearer and healthier communication. It dives a little deeper into what it means to be on the same page as your partner. It's essential on both ends of the relationship. If we can't see something from the other person's perspective whether we're at odds or not, we don't need to be together.

If I had a top five list, this is what my list would look like. Of course it goes on, but these are some of the essentials I take into consideration when I'm interested in somebody. I'm definitely open to dating. I don't stop it, it's just that if you decide to slide a message in a DM or you approach me in public trying to kick your best game, you have to be talking about something. I'm no longer naive to the truth of knowing what I deserve. I refuse to settle for anything less than what I'm worth. I now know how to recognize the difference between a man actually interested in getting to know me and a man whose main goal is to eventually get me in his bed. Upon the first introduction, I have to be able to feel like I'm being introduced to a person with values, goals, amazing characteristics such as being a gentleman and kindhearted. I know you're reading this and feel like that's a lot to take in when you meet someone, but trust me, people will tell you who they are. Most of the time this is revealed through actions, but very rarely is it with words. Of course people want you to have a great first impression of them when you meet them, so they'll tell you anything. However, it's up to you to open your eyes and see past that in order for people to really show you their true colors. I've finally opened my eyes to that, so guys can no longer camouflage themselves around me.

Naked *(10/31/2021)*

I'm sorry to tell you this, but I'm not perfect
Sometimes you'll get mad at me and I'll deserve it
I know what you may have heard, but I'm here to teach you what you should learn
Some days I feel like I'm untouchable
I'll feed you breakfast in bed, I'm at your service
We'll laugh and forget about anything that's concerning
I'll be everything you need
Then there are times where I feel like I'm not worth it
I question how much you care about me
I forget about all the times that you helped me
I let all the nights I shed a tear without you cloud what you really mean to me
I've moved on from my past, but every now and then I get sad
I can't believe that shit had the audacity to happen to me
I don't trust any man and by any, some days that may include you
I said it once, I already told you I got issues that I'm working through
That doesn't mean it still doesn't hurt that he tried me
It still hurts that those other females he was fucking with had the nerve to come for me
It still hurts that these same people chose to lie to me
Sometimes I go back to the days before we met
I channel all those emotions before I had the chance to be open
My anger is sometimes misdirected toward you
Sometimes it's gonna leave you confused
Just know that I'm working towards the betterment of me for you
Sometimes it doesn't take a team
Sometimes I gotta go through shit that only involves me
I don't give up vulnerability freely
That shit got me slapped in the face one too many times
I refuse to go back to the place where I no longer reside
In order to grow, sometimes you have to bare all and show your soul
Sometimes I don't make sense
Sometimes I'll have you questioning exactly who you're fucking with
I'm gonna test your patience
You're gonna have to teach me how to do this, I'm just saying
I'm willing to try because I know I deserve to be loved
And I deserve that love to come from you
This is my truth, and I hope you love me naked just as I love you

**Naked is such a beautifully written song that's as vulnerable as it gets. It's actually another one of my favorite songs I've listened to thus far by Ella Mai. It's just her heart on a page and I love that.*

Better *(11/03/2021)*

Honestly, I don't know why you keep coming back to me
You tell me that you need me and you can't leave
You said if I love you enough, I would give you a second chance
Although I hate that you're not my man, I don't think I can
Please understand the consequence of sleeping with her
That's something I could never forgive, let alone forget
I knew you weren't ready for a relationship
I just wanted you to love me enough to try with it
I made you better, but you made me bitter
I had enough, and though I'm fed up
I still held it down for you, but you wouldn't let up
I'm not staying around just to have you let me down again
I made you better, but you made me bitter
I wish I could forgive you
But that'll only be doing you a favor

Sometimes it hurts, to know that you downsized my worth
You know a picture is worth a thousand words
So when I see you and her together doing more than just work
All I can do is keep it to myself
Saying something to you in that very moment wouldn't help
What you did, you know you were dead wrong
I can't forgive just for you to go back and be with her
The time I thought I had with you
You had been wanting to give to her
She played softly in the background on the strings of your heart
Every time I thought I had you with me
You always said she meant nothing
Yet here I am saying, "Silly of me."

I don't know why, I choose to let you in time after time
You showed to be temporary but convinced me that you were mine
I'm not sure who you are now, but I can't fuck with your kind
I know how embarrassed I felt, can't keep that to myself
I didn't need her help, to make you leave on your own
You took our house and turned it into her home
Yet somehow I still made you better
Even though I had enough, it feels like I'll never be fed up
Because I still held you down but you ain't let up
So I can no longer stay around just to have you let me down
I made you better, but you made me bitter
I wish I could forgive you
But that'll only be doing you a favor

Jaded *(11/06/2021)*

Sometimes it's too hard to let go
Of all the things that I should've never known
Like heartbreak and scars from the pain of the past
Over situations I knew wouldn't last
Now I'm just too used to it
I take my time but I'm not new to this
The honeymoon phase comes in stages
It's only a little bit at a time and then it changes
After all is said and done, I spread my legs and after you're done
You'll walk away
Without too much to say
Sometimes you do the trick
Sometimes I'm so numb I can't even feel it
Sometimes it's hard for me to just have fun
Let me grab my tears and put on a coat of my fears
Because you'll be gone by sunset
Gotta put my mind on reset
Gotta take my time, like this time I'll do it right
Yet I'm here again and still I'm over it
Another sad love song, another piece of my heart gone
My emotions run away with my mind and there's no holding back
Here we go all over again

Heartbreak *(11/06/2021)*

I still remember the days that you loved me
Gave you all my love, you ain't deserve me
I put you on pedestals and gave you everything, I'm too memorable
For you to erase without a thought of me crossing your mind
Where's your escape, baby?
I might be hurt over you, but if it's about who'll lose
It's clear after I heal I could do without you
Without me, you'll be stuck and confused
I can't believe I chose to get my heart broken by you
It's sad but it's true
That you'll never find somebody who loves you the way that I do
How could you leave me to fend for myself?
I told you how I felt abandoned the first time you just up and left
Maybe if you blocked me it would be better
You still let me have access to you, like you would ever answer
I know you see the phone calls and messages of me praying that you'll get better
I'm just saying, I could never leave you down and out
Even if I wanna cuss you out
You must find this amusing
Abusing my heart and leaving me with the bruises
I try to have hope that one day you'll come through for me
I still don't know what I did to make you forget that I even exist
The truth is I could never find it in my heart to do you like this
I wanna say fuck everything we had
I wanna move on, but this pain, this shit hurts so bad
What's even more sad is that you almost loved me back
When you finally came to that realization, that's when you started to retract
This heartbreak is something that I can't fake
One day you'll look back and realize the real tears that I cried
You'll regret ever giving up on all that we had
I know they say time heals all but there's just some shit you just can't get back
I wanna hate you because loving you is just as bad
If you can hear me, I hope one day you'll learn to never do this again
You're back again, but we could never be friends
You let that fly out the window the day you chose to hurt me and pretend
Like I was tripping for my health and you were never wrong for doing me wrong
I could go on about all the things you made me feel
You said I was collateral damage and you couldn't see us together
I can't believe I let you get away with half of the shit I told myself I would do better with
After the last nigga played with me like I wasn't that bitch
It's hard for me to see past this
If you can hear me, just know that karma's the real bitch

Honesty *(11/07/2021)*

A lot of times it's too hard to give what I give
I wish I was stronger
In two years I've faced too much bullshit to be dealing with half-ass actions
I got a few bumps and bruises, but that only adds to me being human
I know it's not easy for you to see me the way that you do
I'm in pain but I'm not ashamed to admit what I've been through
Honestly, I want honesty, and from there let's play it cool
I'm over romance and holding hands and shit out of the unusual
I've invested enough time in too many lies to be with you
I'm not bulletproof, I didn't ask you to make your move
I ain't ask you to aim or shoot, so why'd you have to?
I ain't gon' believe shit that you say to me, that's just how I do
I'm running away from the truth
That's that you love me, and would hold it down no matter what I do
I'm just frontin', about you meaning nothing, because I know that you do
It's just funny, because I want you to see the love in my eyes when I look at you
I want you to feel the passion that I give when I come through
I'm just numb to this, and ain't no coming back from it
It doesn't feel like it used to
I gave away my heart too soon
I gave away my love to the wrong ones that came before you
I'm disconnected from my love
I can't give it to you, let alone just anyone
What I'm missing is probably you, but I can't test that theory to be true
I can't say I want you like you want me
Getting too attached ain't no longer for me
I'm still his best but that doesn't comfort me
I'm a beautiful mess, but I'm trying to clean up for myself

Conversations with the Poet: Story Behind "Heartbreak"

College Dude was the most serious heartbreak I've ever had, but my second situation was the most fatal. In this second situation, I was involved with somewhat of an older guy. He was about five, going on six years older than me. Normally, my age range is no more than three years older than me, but for this particular person, I took a chance in a new direction. The situation had started when I was twenty about to turn twenty-one and he was turning twenty-six. I remember the first day we officially/unofficially met. We kept staring at each other but we would never say more than two words to each other. I'm the one that kind of carried things along with him and took the initiative to make things between us more than just flirty stares and conversations. I ended up sliding him my number, but then I found out he threw it away. I was embarrassed and upset at the same time because why would you do that in front of me? It was technically when I walked away, so I guess he felt like I didn't see it but I did. If you weren't interested, just say that. My bubble got busted even more when I found out from a mutual friend we ended up sharing that he had a girlfriend. That's when the dots connected a little bit on why he rejected my number, but the way he did it still had me in my feelings a little bit. Our mutual friend also let me know they were in a really rocky place. Regardless of the rocky space, I knew for a fact that once I heard girlfriend, I was removing myself from the equation completely and for a while, I stopped acknowledging him.

As time went on, I started back messing with College Dude for the second time around which led to the pregnancy scare. I confided in New Situation about it, but I wasn't aware that this was around the time he was ending his current relationship. He didn't admit to me until after we started our situation that he felt some type of way about me being with somebody else. When I found out I wasn't pregnant, things between College Dude and I drifted apart. To get over College Dude and make me forget what we had, I started this new situation with the older guy. The only problem was even after the pregnancy scare, my relationship with College Dude may have ended, but we were still back and forth with our feelings about each other. New Situation ended up breaking up with his girlfriend and around the time our mutual friend had told me, I was on the outs with College Dude. I started something with New Situation and for a little while it was like a toss up between College Dude and New Situation. I can admit for maybe the first couple of months it was a little triangle situation between me, New Situation, and College Dude. My heart was with College Dude but I had these new feelings that started to develop for this fresh start I was getting with New Situation.

To make a long story short, College Dude ended up with someone else around the time of Valentine's Day. That caused me to cut ties with him completely. From that point forward, I put my focus on myself and New Situation. Since I didn't give myself any time to heal from College Dude, I was looking to latch on to the next best distraction from the pain I was feeling from being hurt in the same way all over again. The only thing is, I chose to give more of what I didn't even have anymore in myself to this new situation. I ended up actually loving New Situation and I started to realize this was much more than us enjoying each other's company. I wanted a committed relationship out of this, however, I wanted what I wanted when I wanted, but he was still holding on to his ex and so was I.

He's a very amazing man. He'll give you the shirt off his back if you need it. He's very sweet, very kind, however he hurt me in a different kind of way than College Dude that I feel is worse than College Dude having multiple females on the side while selling me a committed, monogamous relationship. New Situation tapped into a different kind of pain. He abandoned me. No explanation. Still to this day I haven't heard one word from him and I have no idea what I did to him, and honestly, it's probably best it ended that way for what it was. He opened a deeper wound that everyone who knows me knows not to tap into and those are the abandonment issues that developed via my father, but that allowed me to finally dive into those issues and work on them. New Situation is one of those types of men that if he's going through something, he shuts out the world and keeps to himself and figures it out on his own. I'm very understanding of this because I know he's not used to people being there for him, but at the same time, he never tried to adjust.

Heartbreak is just expressing me being over all of that. New Situation and I keep going in these cycles of these periods of us not speaking at all. I try to give it space, I try to accommodate his feelings, but I've gotten to a point where I'm starting to notice I'm only good for just that with New Situation–accommodating his feelings. This poem was one of those days where I was angry and I had a lot to get off my chest. I'm not heard face to face when it comes to New Situation, so all I can do is write it out. I get tired of trying to convey my emotions when I can only say how I feel when it's convenient to the person. I'm no longer upset. I just honestly can never look at New Situation the same. We were friends before anything and he betrayed my trust without even blinking twice right after I had opened up to him about everything I had been through with College Dude. No conversation needs to be had. Everything happens for a reason. I feel like *Heartbreak* to date is just a poem where I feel like I'm expressing my most current feelings toward him. It's difficult, but the feelings I have towards him at this point are nonexistent.

Scars and All *(11/11/2021)*

Here I am, standing right here in front of you, baby
Just as I am, just as I was yesterday
Today, I hope you can see the changes
I hope the work I put in for myself doesn't go in vain
I hope you see the day to day revisions I put into myself
I'm working on myself, not for you
Only for me, and the only thing I need for you to see
Is that I may be beautifully broken
But I'm becoming completely whole again
God gave me everything I needed to start over again
So I hope you can love me, scars and all
Others got to me before you
I gave them a chance at my heart, but they didn't cherish it
Please be understanding, to the fact that some days I don't know where my head's at
I try not to come at you sideways
My emotions are just like the highways
Giving you the blues with too much traffic on my worst days
Sometimes the speed limit changes
I promise I'm not like this always
It's just while working through the pain, every now and then I still feel some type of way
I just want you to know, that my love is real
I don't take you for granted, my wounds just aren't fully healed
So understand, scars and all, this is who I am
Take me as I give what's no longer left of myself to you

Letter to my Future Husband (11/12/2021)

Dear Lover,

Can we do this again? Can you promise to never stop being my homie, lover, and friend? I don't need a SuperMan. I saved myself once before, I don't need to do it again. I just need you by my side, through thick and thin to the very end. I want us to feel alive and touch the sky like we're floating on cloud nine. Let's never let this flame die between us. Let's fall in love over and over again and make sure nothing can come between us. So just tell me again, that we'll stay lovers and friends. You're the father of my children and with you this life I'm building is bigger than us. We have to make sure we understand the master plan. On our own we'll always shine but together we should stand for one another. Even through the arguments, there's no room for breakups. It's only kisses and makeup. We sometimes wonder if this is really worth it. We're not perfect, but I promise when we continue to put the work in, we'll realize that we're meant to be together our whole lives. To have you holding me at night makes me forget all the times before you when I was cold, alone, and didn't have the right man to call home. All the tears I cried from the mistakes I made, makes me send praises to the most high because I actually made it. Damn, I was distressed and pressed for all the wrong reasons, until the day that I met you and you introduced me to a new season. I remember when it was hard to believe that I could get some relief in my heart. All the heartbreaks, heartaches, and pain prepared me for the day I got the chance to look you in your eyes and swear with my hand on the bible that I'll love you for life. It's true, I'm yours always and forever, down for you no matter the weather. It's me and you, ten toes down. It's never a question. I thank God every day He prepared us for this blessing.

Love,
Yours

Freedom of Self (11/13/2021)

Twenty-one years down and I'm still learning lessons
Sometimes it's hard to find the blessings when you're so caught up in the distractions
Of the pain and the mental state of abandonment
I was abandoned at a young age and it happened again a few months ago
The difference between me now and when I was eight years old is that I'm all about me and what's best for myself
The freedom of self lightens the load better than what I couldn't help
I freed myself from the negativity that came from the love I had for all my enemies
Their words were bond and all the shit they talked was directed to me
I believed everything and was in the mirror coming down on the bitch I thought I was
Until I recognized the crown and realized other people saw my worth
Pressure makes diamonds and I'm ready to kill with guns blazing
My sex appeal too real and for too long I had the nerve to be ashamed of the body and face God gave me
This shit is effortless, and I can't believe all these years I've been so sick of myself and the talent I possess
I can't believe I had regrets on the decisions that I made
I'm gifted and uplifted in every way
I came to change the world with my words that are written and spoken
I'm passionate and open
With every page you turn, you'll fall deeper into the details of my story
Now I'm taking my throne at the table that my hands made
This is for the comeback and the hustles I stacked and for all the motivation I lacked
I let go of what was and now it's time to double up and match the energy I exude to you on a daily that I know you're not used to
This ain't make believe, I'm no longer a dream
This is reality and I'm taking my time
Fine as wine, I'm on my way to the top, and trust me I'm not gon' stop
This is real

All That I Am *(11/13/2021)*

Sometimes it's hard for me to face the fact that I'm still changing
So although you want to love me in my current state
I've loved in many different ways
Every part of me has been taken
For you to expect me to have anything left is selfish and beyond anything I can give you
Because all that I am, could never be all that you are
Although I stand just as tall, too many times I had to catch myself when I fell
What makes you think I'd ever trust you to keep me
Over and over again, I've held my heart in my hands
I already gave it away, I don't want it again
I tried to be a forever, one too many forevers
Now it's only temporary, because my heart is something I no longer carry
All that I am, is not all that I was
I once loved without conditions, now I'm asking for permission
All that I am, seems so far away
Who I really am is finding shelter
My heart is in its case
I know you think you have the answer to my pain, but it's just not the same
All that I am, shouldn't be what you want
I need help from myself, I'm not at my best
Give me time to fix this mess

Conversations with the Poet: Story Behind "All That I Am"

I'm the most impatient person in the world. God knows it. I know it. My family knows it. I expect everything to happen instantly. It doesn't matter what it is or who I'm expecting something from. With that kind of mentality that was hard to break, I faced a lot of challenges. One of those challenges was finding myself in situations like the ones I've shared with you where expectations were never needed in the first place. With everything that's gone on, I've realized that expecting a person to be a certain way or do certain things will always leave you in disappointment. If you expect someone to be the best version of themselves immediately without trying to accept the version of them in front of you, you're leaving nothing but room for them to fall short of your expectations. Another challenge I faced that speaks to my impatience is trying to understand that everything takes time.

All That I Am discusses the struggle of me recognizing that it's difficult for me to accept the fact that I'm still changing. I'm still healing. I'm still growing. Through those realizations, in the poem I'm addressing the person by saying it's wrong for them to expect me to love fully when I don't have too much of myself left to give. It's wrong for them to yearn for my trust when I don't have any at the moment. There's a line specifically that is a testament to myself when I say, "I know you think you have the answer to my pain, but it's just not the same." There was a time where I felt like I could solve everybody's problems, especially with the dude I was involved with. A great example of this is when I was with New Situation.

Throughout the ups and downs of us going through the motions for a little over a year, New Situation faced a lot of challenges that I never realized were above me. Towards the end of our situation, he had taken a lot of loss, and one of them in particular I was the first person he texted and called about it because he said I was the only person he wanted to speak with about it. Then he ended up losing someone else who was very close to him. After that he ended up losing a high school friend, and it just seemed like to him and from the outside looking in nothing would ever be okay at the time. I felt like I could be that person to make everything okay. However, with experiencing grief myself, I understand that there's really nothing that can be done by anybody to make you feel absolutely okay. I beat myself up about that a lot because I felt like I wasn't doing enough in those times. When he was pushing me away and shutting me out, I felt like I could force him to let me in and be his shoulder to cry on. Unfortunately, I was ruling out the fact that this was the process of grief. I wasn't stepping outside of myself and my feelings to see the bigger picture, which was above anything I could provide. That was something that had to be left in God's hands.

Aside from that, when he felt like he didn't want to do music anymore, I felt like I could be an inspiration and an encouragement to push him back into that. When he faced a point where he was going through other things legally, I thought me being there for him through every step of that would allow him to see me for what I should be to him. I just felt like I could do a lot for situations that were not in my control.

All That I Am is me letting go of that control and manipulation of time as well as my expectations. This is why I end it with "give me time to fix this mess," because for so long I've been patching up the issues instead of taking time to clean up the wounds and give them the proper time to heal. They may not necessarily look entirely the same once they heal, but the healing process is vital. Taking your time is vital, and the stress of expectations isn't necessary.

Issues *(10/28/2021)*

Your heart isn't supposed to be a battlefield of unhealed scars
It seems ever since I figured out what love is, I'm back and forth with
fighting against the scars and opening my heart
A wounded soldier at best, I let my broken heart take care of the rest
I'm fearless with my guard up, ain't no S on my chest
I'm tired of mending broken souls just so they can take advantage of the fact
that I love hard but my loyalty go harder
Through all the frustration and hesitation, I'm ready to ride
We ain't gon' die 'cause I got my nine hangin' from the whip
The wheels might fall off but I'm still riding the stick
I'm confident, in whatever I got going on with the one that I'm with

Yet somehow I still find a way to get the short end of the stick
Somehow I can't convince myself that this one's not it
I give my all and choose to blame the one that I'm with
When really I saw the signs, I just got used to playing pretend
I didn't want it to end
I thought if I just made it known that I wanted to be more than friends
Then maybe we could push aside the problems and be lovers again
I got it bad and I know it
Even though I hate to show it
Romance is where my issues lie, I can't run from it
So let me dump this here

Wishful Thinking *(10/29/2021)*

I could keep my pen to the page, because how I feel about you is endless
I'm always around to save the day, because for you I'll make the world stop
Just to make it all seem okay
Sometimes the shit that you go through is out of my hands
Still I try to be there for you the best way that I can
I'll be your shoulder for all the tears that you shed
My door is always open when you wanna escape
I'm not opposed to all the love that we make
When you have to release those frustrations only your body can discuss
I just wish I was as important to you as you are to me
I wish I could be your everything despite your fears
I wish you weren't so scared to trust that together we'll be everything that we need to be
Truth is it hurts me that you still treat me like a groupie
One minute I'm your girl and the next you're pushing back on me

I wish I could open your eyes to see your heart is safe in my hands
I wish you could understand every time you abandon me, you remind me of him
We both got issues and scars from the past
The difference between me and you is that I'm not carrying burdens that last
You use that shit as an excuse to keep your heart on what you used to have
If you're so stuck on what she did, go back to where you belong
I love you but if you wanna be with me, I don't have time for the back and forth
I don't have time for you to keep changing your mind when I know you're not alone
It's twisted how manipulative you turned out to be
I can't believe I ever staked my love on the man I thought you were to me
Once you leave, ain't no coming back to me
You better believe when a woman's fed up, that's really when the story ends
I'm putting my feelings for you to bed, I hope you understand what you just did
So much for wishful thinking

One of Those Days *(11/16/2021)*

It's one of those days for me
Why does this have to be so familiar to me?
I thought I did everything to erase you from my heart
We've been here before, but somehow the love is stronger
Fire and desires, burning underneath the surface
I gave everything the last two times I thought you were mine
How could you do this to me?
I moved on for the better but now I'm questioning where my head's at
I never would've thought we would be here
Look in my eyes and you can see clearly
The pain you tossed my way
It's one of those days where I know I'm not ever gonna be the same
Am I going backwards or is this what comes after growth?
I'm tired of going out and not finding what I deserve
Am I being tested or is this new version of you someone I should get to know?
I'm tired of giving love and not finding what's best for me
Since you keep coming back to me, does that mean we're meant to be?
I'm out of my mind, but it's something inside I can't believe exists in my heart for you
Forever, we are one
I've played this game before and you left me in the dust
How am I supposed to be now that you're still here?
I'm tired of giving love and being left to feel empty
This feels good but I know better than to reminisce on what we were
Too much on my mind to understand what's really your plan
Is this temporary or are you fully committed?
A recurring absence is something my heart can no longer take
I'm feeling like anything and everything has an ulterior motive
I'm not broken but I'm far from being wholesome
It's hard for me to know what's really the deal with you
Are we chill or are you using me to make yourself feel better?
Are you still hiding from what you know you need to do better?
Too many unanswered questions for me to trust this even just a little bit
I'm tired of giving love and being left alone
All the while I'm living under the reality of a cliche
Of the hopeless romantic who can't keep her heart at bay
So it's hard to believe you but this feels so right
It's one of those days
I'm open on the inside but outside I'm losing my mind
On a high from what we shared last night
Should I believe in our good days?

Too Hard *(11/16/2021)*

It's hard to believe anything you say to me
You've never been a master of consistency
One minute I'm on your mind and you're racing against time
Tryna find ways for you to be mine
Then in the blink of an eye, you say you never meant for things to get too far
Never meant to get your feelings involved

Still I can't get you out of my head
Here we go doing the same dance again
Before, the music was fading in the background and we were driven further apart
Now our moves are in sync and I don't want them to stop
Love isn't supposed to live here anymore
I thought when I closed that door, you wouldn't come back anymore
It's too hard and relationships seem so far away from me
Maybe it's right here waiting with you and me

Open Book *(11/17/2021)*

I said it was over but now I'm not sure anymore
I've gotten over you yet here you are at my front door
With a bruised ego and pride you had to let go
So many apologies, I don't even know if they're for sure

You confessed your love for me with my head on your chest
Said I was the only one you could turn to whenever in distress
I possessed everything you were looking for
I was your best
It's funny how you admit your true feelings after a year of no loving from me
I removed myself from you but you were yearning to come back to me

You say you should've never let me go
Said you wouldn't be where you are now if you would've gave us a chance
I wanted you as my man, but you had other plans
You thought she had everything you needed at a glance

Now you're looking for affection from me with no love loss
A closer connection without the extra cost
I tried to give it to you twice but you didn't want to see me through
The tables turned and now you regret what you did
You know I love you but it's hard to forget
How I wasn't your main priority
Or how you chose her over me

Conversations with the Poet: Story Behind "Issues"

When I'm with somebody, I'm *with* that person 100%. There's no in between. I really take the statement 'go hard or go home' with my love life to heart, because in my mind I feel like that's how it should be. I'm the ride or die chick. Hell no, I'm not about to go to jail for you and we're not dying, but I am about to make sure I hold it down for you in a way that keeps you from going that route. You've got certain career goals, let's figure out a plan and how we can execute that so you can reach your fullest potential. When you're going through something emotionally and mentally, I'll be the one that's ready to do whatever I can to make you laugh and smile to take your mind off of the pain as long as I can. However, in the same token, I'm also that listener that you need to vent about your problems as well as that encouragement that you seek when you feel like the walls are closing in. I'm the giver in the absolute highest form when it comes to my man.

Issues is me addressing how much I'm over giving that part of myself to the ones that I think deserve it and it comes back to slap me in the face. While writing this poem, I'm addressing multiple situations at once again. That first stanza I started off conflicted. I'm in between feeling like a wounded animal trying to lick her wounds clean to patch myself up enough to try again. In the same token, I'm also afraid and guarded with trying to be open enough to have a new connection enter my life. As I transition from the pain and the trauma of certain situations like my abusive situation, I now have the tossup of wanting to be in a relationship but also being fed up with the idea of being in one because I don't want to continue to get hurt. Once you go through that cycle of being heartbroken over and over and the scenarios get worse and worse every time, it makes you not only hesitant but also fearful.

Issues speaks to the fact that I'm tired of being in a space where I'm prone to bullshit. It's hard for me to see the signs that are clearly right in front of my face because I want things between me and the person I'm with to work a certain way. I had an unhealthy obsession with forcing situations to be what I wanted them to be. For example, with College Dude the first time around, I knew he wasn't ready to be in a relationship, let alone a relationship with me. I saw all the signs of him still holding on to the pain of his ex by how he chose to constantly reminisce about what she did. It made things extremely awkward and uncomfortable for me by how much he always mentioned her. Since the three of us went to the same school, it became even more difficult because when we crossed paths with her I could sense the tension but also see the attraction that was still between them. I knew he wasn't 100% with me, but I tried to convince myself that I could make him be all in. I didn't realize that pressure and me forcing him to try to be something that he wasn't meant to be put a weight on our situation that couldn't be carried. I did the exact same thing with New Situation.

As the poem continues on, I end it with "so let me dump this here" to kind of let it be known that deep down I didn't want to carry the burden of this pain and these issues alone. I wish I could drop some of them off at the doorstep of the person who these problems are rooted from. In no way am I trying to dismiss the fact that some of my issues start with myself and the choices I made along the way. However, it does speak to the fact that I wish I could go to the source of the pain for certain things and address it with this person or these particular people. Especially with New Situation. How things ended between us was very unfortunate, and the way it ended makes me believe that we may never cross paths again because he'll do everything in his power to avoid it. He made it clear when he made his dramatic exit that he wasn't necessarily ready nor would he ever be ready to have that conversation of where it went wrong and how it made me feel. I have so many emotions and frustrations toward him that I want to express, and I think he knows that, which is why he won't ever allow me to communicate them to him directly face to face. Therefore, I have to force myself to let go and move on so those "issues" developed through him don't turn into defense mechanisms used against guys that could possibly be nothing like him.

Lady in the Glass Dress *(N.D)*

Meet the lady in the glass dress
Here lies her pain
She waltz inside the darkest room and you can still see her veins
They lead you to her broken heart
Lady in the glass dress, where do you remain?
Do you realize that your journey is filled with nothing but pain?
Even on her best days, she still finds it hard to smile without a strain
She's under distress

Lady in the glass dress, who are you?
Where lies your truth and what will you get into?
Where will you be?
Who will you become?
It seems to me as if your story will always remain undone
Your start is never your finish
Your end seems to always be another beginning

Lady in the glass dress, what lies beyond thy self?
What is your worth?
What can you become?
For that is unknown
You're lost in the shadows, broken and distrubed
You've disappeared while life goes on around you
You're in despair and sit in your sorrows at night

Lady in the glass dress, guess what? I am you
You're a part of me that I just can't shake loose
You've become my weakness, something I see straight through
Against all odds, I still have you
I want you gone because you can't stay
Even when I try to push you away, you still remain my biggest mistake
My motivation and self esteem as a young woman all gets erased

**Shoutout to Chris Brown. The line of his song, Lady in a Glass Dress, stayed on repeat in my head when I was writing this. It goes, "Lady in the glass dress, I can see right through you." I used that and just expanded on it more from my own perspective.*

Benevolence *(11/18/2021)*

I got your letter today
You addressed it to the home you knew once before
Too bad the girl you used to know doesn't live there anymore

You pinned your farewell to the broken pieces of my heart
You got offended because I compared you to the man that left me broken from the start
How is it my fault that I felt abandoned when you chose not to play your part?
You said life took over for you and you ain't have space for me in your heart

You said I should've known better since I know how you are
You gave yourself permission to go back and forth with my true feelings
You couldn't keep it consistent
Yet somehow you blamed me for not putting up with it

You say you understand where I'm coming from when I give you my grief about how we've been dealing
Then you turn around to put the nail in the coffin
With your gun in hand, you shoot me down like from the start, you had a plan
To ruin me to the very end, so we could never really begin
No, we are not friends, and the bond will never be what it was
You say you don't want to hold me back from reaching my fullest potential
Who are you to know when I'll finally peak?
Who's to say you missed your beat and I was already at full capacity
It's funny how you had the audacity to type away in your feelings
Long paragraphs and you blocked me before I could get my input in
You ain't say it to my face because you couldn't handle the position you put me in
You didn't want to deal with the repercussions that went with doing me wrong
Yet somehow you don't want to see me with nobody else
You went ghost on me twice and both times I still stayed by your side
I guess it hits different when love turns out not to be two-sided

You wished me the best but you took a dramatic exit
I thought I had the best of you but turns out, I was being served leftovers
I had to move on, you gave me no other option
If I ever saw you on the street, I would probably keep walking
There's nothing left to say
Once you gave your goodbyes, you already picked a side
Once I saw it wasn't mine, I knew I had to let the romance die
I lost all respect for the man I thought you were to date

Now I don't settle
Fuck a commitment, the heartache is endless, I should win a gold medal for pretending
Like I moved on from the past, acting like the present is filled with good vibes that'll last
I figured if I hated you more, I could love you a little less

You had what I wanted, but it looks like I needed something different
Now I'm back to being numb and selfish with a small case of conceited
Things are complicated, immature, and I'm a little more confused
But one thing I forced myself to do was forget about you
I'm not in the mood, to walk down a bunch of memories that you made clear to me
They ain't mean that much to you
If I'm being honest, I was sparing you, I just hoped you returned the favor
I thought it could work both ways
Dearly beloved, I know you ain't love me, and if you were wondering
About their being love lost between us
Just know that before I wake, hopefully you pray
That I have mercy on your heart, since there ain't no love on my part

Supposedly *(11/21/2021)*

You tried to leave me, broken and confused
You knew that I loved you, and that I'd do anything for you
So when you up and left with no explanation, you knew I would be hurt and bruised
Supposedly, my world revolves around you
So you thought once you removed yourself, I wouldn't know what to do
You thought I would be drowning in my tears
You thought you left me with all these fears to ever love someone again
Thought I would swear I'd never open my heart to anyone outside of you
This just goes to show that you never really knew me
If you did, you would already know that I stand tall, especially on my own
I was whole before I met you, so please believe me when I say I'm moving on
I'll be even better now that you're gone
Supposedly, I'm supposed to regret the day I met you and be bitter
There you go not understanding that my heart has no room to hate you
Supposedly, I'm supposed to be running back to you
Unfortunately, I cannot seem to find a reason to

**Shout out to Heather Headley. "Ain't It Funny" is definitely the truth and it's been proven multiple times that everything she says in that song is exactly how it is in real life.*

Round 3 *(11/22/2021)*

You came running back to me all on your own
I didn't ask you to stay, you're the one that got comfortable
You want me to promise I'll never walk away again
You claim the last time it happened, you felt too much pain
You want me to tell you again, that I promise to be your homie till the end
Cautiously, you choose to love me, but in the back of your mind, you know it's too late
I refuse to get my hopes up for you, because we've played this game before
You're the one that left me standing at the door
I won't beg you to hold on to me anymore

I can't really say, I'm numb to the pain
I've always loved you in my heart anyway
Now you're choosing to confess all your feelings to me
Why did I have to leave for you to realize what you were losing?
The questions are endless, but I don't feel the need to ask
I already know the answer, and it would piss me off if you said anything other than that
My feelings magnified with my healing, is something I can't take back
So here we are once again, trying to regain our strength and get back on track

Conversations with the Poet: Story Behind "Benevolence"

I love Wale. I *love* Wale. He's so underrated it's crazy. He's a super dope lyricst to me, and how poetic he is on certain records just draws me in every time. My favorite song by him that I can keep on repeat is *Illest Bitch*. That song got me through a lot of the low points in my life when I first introduced myself to it, and it still gets me through some of my bad days to this day. However, another song that kinda hit close to my heart is one from his most recent project he just released, *Folarin II*, and it's called *Dearly Beloved*. In the song, he samples a song from The Jamie Foxx Show also called *Dearly Beloved*. I love Jamie Foxx all around, and when I was younger I was a faithful fan of *The Jamie Foxx Show.* Outside of the wedding song he performed, *Dearly Beloved* is my favorite song he ever sang on that show. The two coming together was cold as hell to me, but outside of that, the lyrics are what stuck with me the most. After listening to the song on repeat for weeks, I ended up starting to form my own opinion on what I felt like it was about. What I ended up taking away from it was it addressed a potential lover who things could never quite work out with because of so many outside influences that came in between what was developing between them. The person moved on and is in a committed relationship, and Wale is basically telling that person don't forget about what they had. The woman ended up with someone else, but her heart was still with him. Unfortunately, the circumstances surrounding them kept them apart. Timing wasn't right. That reminded me of my connection with New Situation and College Dude.

This poem is a response to a message New Situation had sent me a few months back. This was the very last day I heard from him. Before he sent that message, he had gone weeks without responding to any of my phone calls, voicemails, text messages. Nothing. However, before he went ghost, we spent every single day together. Everything was fine, so I was confused as to why all of a sudden I wasn't hearing anything from him. Fast forward a couple weeks, he sends me this long four page letter message basically telling me he wasn't good enough for me and he felt like he was dragging me down with him. He said we just needed to stop and that was it. He blocked me on everything and there was no clear explanation of why that happened. When I got this message, I was at my mom's house. After I read it, I went into her room and cried like a baby. She came in there and asked me if I was okay and I just laid my head on her chest and just let it all out. I did that for like an hour, and then she told me to clean myself up and meet her in the living room. That night she gave me the best advice ever. She told me the only reason he sent me that message was because he didn't want to see the reaction I was giving her now in his face. He couldn't handle my tears. She said sometimes men, or people in general, have to step up to the plate when it comes to dealing with other people's emotions, especially in love. If what's required of them is something they don't want to fulfill, they run. However, she also told me either I could sit around and cry while I waited for him to come back, or I could pick myself up and move on. She told me he was content with what he just did because he didn't have to deal with how emotional I was at that moment.

I was tired of crying about the situation, so I just started writing, and then I listened to *Dearly Beloved* again. That's what created the poem you guys just read. I'm very grateful I wrote this poem because if I hadn't, I would probably have a lot of hatred in my heart towards New Situation. I've tried my best not to hate anybody no matter what they do to me because I don't have room for it, but that was a time where if I hadn't taken the time to get everything out in the moment, I would've grown to hate him. Whatever his deal was, that's not on me, and I didn't want the burden of the emotion of hate to be carried on my heart. Me hating him doesn't change anything that happened. It doesn't make me feel better. Me holding the situation and how he handled it against him doesn't make me feel good. Writing about it made me feel better.

Thoughts
Of
A
Sober
Heart

Honest Conversations Pt. 3

Getting your heart broken obviously isn't fun. It's definitely something that's not a game and it shouldn't be treated as one. I try to never play with anybody's feelings because unfortunately I know how that feels all too well. However, I have had situations where I wasn't all in post heartbreak. The other person was in love with me while I was just getting by with them so I wasn't lonely. With some, I forced myself to go along with it because I didn't want to be by myself. Other times I ran from connections that were actually good for me because I tried to convince myself that the person wasn't my type. I kept making the excuse of me not being "ready" for a relationship, when in reality I was, I just had it set in my mind that I wanted a relationship with only one person that was no longer a part of my life. It hurts, but at the same time it's all about how you come back from that. I wrote this collection and did these little inserts to let young women and men know that this love shit hurts to the core a lot of times. When you do get the rareness of it all as far as true love goes, hold on to it as tight as you can. However, for those women and men out there who are hurting, because of heartbreak and not being treated right, first of all, you're not alone. Second of all, you deserve better. You're kings and queens. You deserve to be treated as beautiful as your reflection in the mirror. No exceptions. No one deserved to be treated anything short of amazing

I have a baby sister. She just turned eighteen back in September, and it breaks my heart that she had to be the one outside of my mother on multiple occasions to wipe my tears. I remember a lot of times I was breaking down in her arms and she was giving me encouragement and pep talks. Anybody who knows me knows my sister is my other half for life. I stand ten toes down for her and she does the exact same thing for me. I think when our brothers moved on to life beyond the closeness of the family, our bond got even stronger. She taught me a lot about myself and love, and it just showed me how wise she was at such a young age. At the time I was going through all of this, she was like fifteen or sixteen, so she already had the script together. I want my baby sister to read this and see my strength and be proud that I became more than my pain.

Summer Walker blessed our ears this month with her second album, *Still Over It*. I listened to that from top to bottom, and there wasn't one track that didn't hit for me. What I had on repeat the first time I listened to the album all the way through was the prayer Ciara said at the end to close everything out. In that prayer, one thing that I've been repeating to myself that she said is, "My pain has a purpose." When she first said that, I was a little thrown off. In my mind, I'm like, why would I hurt this much and there be purpose behind it? Why am I purposefully getting hurt? Of course since I was butt hurt, I took it the wrong way. However, once I started taking this journey away from chasing after a man and started running after myself, my eyes started to open more and I realized my pain does have a purpose. This is it. This is the purpose behind my pain. This is one of the reasons why I went through what I went through. This project would've still most likely happened, but it wouldn't have been this beautiful.

Thoughts of a Sober Heart is driven by experiences and music. If I didn't have Summer Walker's *Still Over It* or Queen Naija's *Misunderstood* or Laytone Greene's *Tell Ya Story*, I wouldn't be able to know how to convey how I feel in a way that other people also not only understand but can relate to. If I didn't go through what I went through, I wouldn't have any experiences to talk about. I wouldn't be as open to putting myself out there like I am now. I wouldn't be vulnerable for not just my eyes, but now the whole world's eyes. It's a lot to take in and it's a lot to grasp, but while writing this project, I grew with it. Every step of the way I was evolving to the person I am right here, right now, and I love that for me. I'm proud of myself for putting my all into something I finished, and although I was reliving these experiences line after line, it showed me how far I've come. This is from me to every woman and man out there, and I hope everyone took something from this. I wrote this for the people, and as long as I touch at least one person with this, I'm satisfied.

Thoughts
Of
A
Sober
Heart

Thoughts of a Sober Heart *(10/28/2021)*

Something should've told me, I should've walked away from you
The day you had the nerve to look me in my face and admit my heart was something you would never take
I know you understand, that I gave you everything I had left in me
That's why it's so easy for you to just up and leave me
You took advantage of the fact that I made myself need you for there to be a me
You took for granted that I would do anything just to be next to you at night
When I feel cold, I turn to you the most
You proved time after time, you never had intentions to get that close

Sometimes it hurts me to know that my heart is too fragile for you
Since I'm so desperate to be loved by you, I don't mind being in the shadows
Your dirty little secret, I was, and you tried everything to keep it
You were my reason to love you, because I thought you were my beginning
Only to find out this time you would be my ending
I was hoping I found not just a lover, but a friend in you
Yet here you are telling me again, we mean absolutely nothing to you
Every other day you regret the love we make
How do you expect me to stay when it seems like you feel so ashamed?

If I could take it back for you, I would've never looked your way
Apparently I'm your biggest mistake, that I'm sorry you ever made
Have you ever felt alone sleeping next to the one you love?
It's to the point where I love you with all my heart
I'm just trying not to hate you as much
If I really sit and think about it, you were never mine from the start
You kept telling me you couldn't break away from the pain that she caused
You said she made it hard for you to ever wanna be with somebody else
Now I see you didn't really wanna be with anybody because she left

Here we are a year into this, and you're still playing out of tune
Somebody took everything I had once before, but somehow I still chose you
This is how it feels to give to someone who doesn't deserve you
Foolish of me to continue to cling to the hope of what he and I could ever be
I was drunk off your touch, feenin' for your lust, but I'll never be enough for you, baby
That's what's so fucked up for me, and I can't explain it, but believe me when I say
I wish I meant something to you, I wish I never meant nothing to you
Even with me standing beside you with everything you put me through
As I look into your eyes, I can see, that still means nothing to you

Thoughts
Of
A
Sober
Heart

"The Playlist"

1. Passionate
2. Conversations
3. Perfectly Imperfect
4. Final Destination
5. Lie To Me
6. Separate Spaces
7. Nevermind
8. Trust Issues
9. Where
10. Want U 2 Fly
11. Reminisce
12. Dream Girl
13. Come Closer
14. Lola
15. Stuck On You
16. So Over It
17. Tables Turn
18. Time Changes
19. Love's Heartbeat
20. Keep Me In Mind
21. My Diary
22. Someday I'll Love Faith Smith
23. Matters Of My Heart
24. Maybe
25. To Me, From You
26. If You Can Hear Me
27. Goodbyes at Sunset
28. Emotions
29. You Got Me
30. Runaway
31. Overrated
32. Perspective
33. Naked
34. Better
35. Jaded
36. Heartbreak
37. Honesty
38. Scars and All
39. Letter to my Future Husband
40. Freedom of Self
41. All That I Am
42. Issues
43. Wishful Thinking
44. One Of Those Days
45. Too Hard
46. Open Book

47. Lady in the Glass Dress
48. Benevolence
49. Supposedly
50. Round 3
51. Thoughts of a Sober Heart

Thoughts
Of
A
Sober
Heart

Faith's Favorites

1. Passionate
2. Lie To Me
3. Separate Spaces
4. Nevermind
5. Where
6. Want U 2 Fly
7. Dream Girl
8. Come Closer
9. Tables Turn
10. Keep Me In Mind
11. My Diary
12. Someday I'll Love Faith Smith
13. Matters Of My Heart
14. Emotions
15. Better
16. Letter to my Future Husband
17. Freedom of Self
18. Issues
19. One of Those Days
20. Benevolence
21. Supposedly
22. Round 3

Discussion Questions

1. Out of the entire collection, what was your favorite piece and why? How did this piece make you feel? What did you take away from it?
2. If you could rearrange the lineup of poems, how would you arrange them and why?
3. *Round 3* is about me giving College Dude one last and final chance. Do you feel people deserve more than one chance when it comes to love? Would you give College Dude a third chance after knowing what he did?
4. What does commitment mean to you? Do you believe our generation of men and women lack the sense of commitment that was exemplified in past generations? Or do you think commitment is still strong, it just depends on the person you're with?
5. There has always been a great debate about monogamous relationships. I'm very big on monogamy and I express that fully throughout the collection. However, as you have read, I've never experienced being a part of a monogamous relationship, because the faithfulness was lacking in all my situations. How do you feel about monogamy? Do you believe it's possible to be with one woman or man and be devoted only to that person? Or do you think the times have changed so much that it's rare to even experience monogamy?
6. *Thoughts of a Sober Heart* speaks to realizing that New Situation was never going to love me the way that I wanted to be loved. Have you ever experienced not being fully loved or not fully loving the person the way that you or they want you to? What was it like?
7. *Conversations* is a piece about mental health and fighting the voices in my head that kept me from loving who I was. I also couldn't fully love the person I was with at the time. Why is it important to have good mental health before involving yourself with someone? Is there a lack of or too much judgment when it comes to mental health? Why or why not?
8. Self love is something that should be practiced daily. Actually, I highly encourage it, because if you can't love yourself, you can't love anybody else. I wrote *Someday I'll Love Faith Smith* as a self-love poem. Name one way you show yourself the most beautiful act of love that you can't get anywhere else. When you name it, ask and answer out loud, why would you ever search for that same form of love you give yourself in anyone else?

Q&A With The Author

Why did you choose to openly discuss past relationships?

I'm a woman first and foremost, but I'm also human. Love doesn't just put certain things on hold because you want it when you want it or because you're hurt. We've all been there before. Every situation I broadly go into detail about somebody has experienced in one form or another. People have had it way worse than me, and I acknowledge that and I understand that, which is why I'm putting a voice to it. I let College Dude read pieces of this while I was going through the drafting process of this collection, so this wasn't a platform to have a tell-all session. Everything that's said within these poems and excerpts are things I would say to the guy I'm addressing face-to-face. Plus, I barely scraped the surface of any situation I discussed, and I did that to protect these individuals' privacy. I'm not about to give out names. I'm not about to take shots, because this wasn't about that. This was simply about presenting a beautiful healing journey to the world in order to help or inspire someone else.

What advice would you give to someone going through similar scenarios in their relationships right now?

Trust your gut. Your gut has never lied to you. Ever. It's never been a time where I was in a situation and I had this gut feeling and it was wrong. I've been in plenty of situations where everything just played out for the worst and I knew I should've listened to my intuition. Queen Naija said it best. Your intuition never lies, and I promise that's the truest thing I've ever heard. If I would have gone with my gut feeling, I probably wouldn't have gone through half of what I did. Do what's best for you.

Also, don't lose yourself in your situation. Going through the motions is difficult. You're unsure about a lot of things. You don't know if the circumstances within the situation are going to get better. It's unpredictable, but the one thing you can hold on to and you can be sure of is yourself. Protect your crown. King or queen, stay sitting on your throne. I've been in positions where I lost myself in the person I was trying to fix things with knowing they weren't going to get better and that I needed to let them go for the betterment of myself. Once you lose yourself in someone amongst the chaos, that's when you get on a roller coaster that's hard to get off of.

What made you incorporate music with your poems?

As you can see throughout the collection, music was the main inspiration outside of my experiences for each piece. That's why I'm giving credits to Wale, Chris Brown, Dream Doll and a bunch of other amazing artists, rappers, and singers. If it wasn't for these artists and their bodies of work, I would be confused as to how to put my emotions on a page the way that I did. Music is the model that I follow. I feel like most of these poems are songs anyway. That's one of the main reasons I decided to title the collection *Thoughts of a Sober Heart*. Of course it has a deeper meaning that I explained in the beginning, but it also sounds like a dope album title that one of my favorite artists like SZA, Summer Walker or Kehlani would drop. In my head, I swear I'm an artist in the music industry (Ha!). I just love music.

Music also helped me through a lot of the heartache. All the songs that I reference are some of the many songs that I listened to while working through my emotions after these situations ended. It's always that one song that just sums everything up for a particular situation. Or that one song that hits your heart in a way that nothing else can. How about that song that makes you feel like you're reliving everything all over again? That's what the music did for me during this time. These songs helped me align with the greater truth behind everything and a clearer understanding on not only what was happening but why it was happening.

CHOOSE

Love

Love me, like a child loves its youth
Hang on to me like it's the only thing you ever wanna do
Love me now
Like tomorrow doesn't exist
If all we have is this moment right here
Love me like we'd be sharing our last kiss
Love me now
Because forever doesn't last too long
So if you're betting on forever
You might as well consider this the end of our song
Love me now

Faith L. Smith was born and raised in Gary, IN. She now resides in Griffith, IN and is currently a Front Desk Attendant at the Hampton Inn and Suites in Schererville. She is currently finishing her Bachelor's Degree in English from Indiana University Northwest.

Contact Information:

E-mail: creativelyfaith21@gmail.com
Instagram: @_creativelyfaith
Twitter: @faithfulvibesss

www.ingramcontent.com/pod-product-compliance
Lightning Source LLC
LaVergne TN
LVHW080043170826
845677LV00024B/1562

* 9 7 9 8 2 1 8 0 4 0 8 2 6 *